On the day I told him I was going to major in journalism (by force of circumstance because I failed math), the artist Ely Santiago, a Beta Sigman who later became a well-known painter and graphic artist, did this sketch of what he saw of my future.

True to her name, Gemma (Nemenzo) proves with *Heart in Two Places* that she is a brilliant writer who can move you to tears as easily as she can move you to laughter with her thought-provoking and insightful essays. Here, the witty essayist proffers a writer's harvest that sparkles with disarming humor (delightfully sprinkled with Pinoy pixie dust) and, to great effect, cuts with hard-edged passion and intelligence.

BERNARDO BERNARDO
Fil-Am Actor/Director

What a delightful collection! Indeed, Gemma Nemenzo writes from two places—from then and now, from laughter and tragedy, and always from a generous heart and unfaltering wisdom.

CRISTINA DC PASTOR
Author, *Scratch the News: Filipino Americans in Our Midst*
Managing Editor, *Philippine News*

The courage that saw Gemma Nemenzo end her marriage, pull up stakes and migrate to America with three young children is the same courage that she trains on herself in this book—a pained, sometimes ironic, sometimes amused record of life as she has since lived it.

Here a staunch nationalist turned U.S. citizen, a female born to relationship raising her children alone, a writer turning separation from her roots into literature—proves her examined life to be truly worth living.

SYLVIA L. MAYUGA
Award-winning journalist

Heart In Two Places goes beyond geographic and cultural bilocation. Between the covers of this book are scintillating vignettes of Gemma Nemenzo's experiential FilAm sojourn.

Ms. Nemenzo's essays are masterfully crafted "sentipieces," much unlike vapid musings that cram less cerebral bookstores. Verbally gifted, she amazes readers with the way her words flow in facile procession: the obvious are precise, while inferences are delicately nuanced. Her versatile pen, as the situation demands, morphs into an incisive scalpel or a blunt bludgeon or, when mortally whimsical, slays nonetheless with the gentle swirl of a scimitar.

Essentially, *Heart in Two Places* is about the author's FilAm life journey, punctuated with defining moments and crucial life choices. In the process, she raises philosophical questions that disturb, yet edify. Somehow, one senses that in her heart of hearts, her life choices are unarguably impelled by a living, breathing, sensitive, considerate soul. Then, perhaps, the book should be retitled *Heart in Right Places*.

RAFAEL "RAY" V. DE GUZMAN
Senior Vice President and Senior Executive Officer
United Laboratories, Inc., Philippines

One cannot read Gemma Nemenzo's essays without being moved to tears or to laughter, or a strong sense of empathy. Or even struck with familiarity with the different faces of human experience she dwells on.

NENI STA. ROMANA CRUZ
Book author

Heart in Two Places

An Immigrant's Journey

Gemma Nemenzo

To Jackie –

with admiration

and gratitude

Gemma

Anvil
Manila

Heart in Two Places: An Immigrant's Journey
by Gemma Nemenzo

Copyright © Gemma Nemenzo, 2007

Published and exclusively distributed by ANVIL PUBLISHING INC.
8007-B Pioneer St., Barangay Kapitolyo, Pasig City 1603 Philippines
Sales & Marketing: 637-3621; 637-5141; 747-1624; marketing@anvilpublishing.com
Fax: 637-6084
www.anvilpublishing.com

First printing, March 2007
Second printing, August 2007

Visuals provided by the author.

Edited by Paulynn P. Sicam

Cover design by Bumper de Jesus and Joe de Jesus
Book design by Ani V. Habúlan

ISBN 978-971-27-1867-0

Printed in the Philippines
By: COR-ASIA, INC.

Foreword

MY MOTHER WAS A MYTHICAL CREATURE to me in my childhood. Aloof and ethereal, she was always engaged in mysterious activities related to the excitement of the revolution; palatable, even if not quite comprehensible, to a child's mind. She returned home late and left early in the morning, and I was fascinated by the small clues of her existence. Late at night I would be awakened by the sound of her typewriter in the next room, the rhythmic banging then a whir as the typewriter shifted to the next line, and I would drift back to sleep, the sound comforting as a lullaby. The next morning I would go to her room and examine the remnants of her words, mirror images left behind on the back of the carbon paper she used to make duplicate copies of her writing, unfinished pages where the last sentence would be shrouded under a line of x's before being discarded.

I would stare at the pictures of her in the living room, captivated by the smile on her face or the distance in her eyes, as I tried to imagine more secret details about her. In her third grade class picture, big-headed with a pristine bowl haircut and a mischievous grin, she sat in a short skirt and knee stockings, distracted and gazing past the camera, waiting to become the woman, effortlessly beautiful and infinitely mysterious.

When we moved to America, the drastically different context created the negative image of her—like film held up to the light, everything white was black and people stared back at you with hollowed out eye sockets and pupils disconcertingly perched at the center. In the Philippines I excused her as being above the tedium of daily chores as she spent most of the day out, doing activities of immense importance while the maids and our beloved *yaya* attended to the cooking and cleaning and fetching us from school. In California I blamed her for never learning how to cook and for feeding us a repetitive cycle of ground beef with peas and baked chicken, neither delicious nor reminiscent of the Filipino food we loved so much. But also while she'd been an aloof and distant mother, built around tales and imaginings, in America she became, if not entirely attentive as she single-handedly juggled jobs and kids, certainly engaged.

Between arguments and long stretches where she worked ceaselessly, were the days we spent scouring the Asian food stores for *queso de bola* and *pan de sal* for Christmas, poring over old pictures retelling shared memories, and laughing at our failed attempts at making *torta* or *biko*. Over the years, as we—my mother, baby sister, older brother, and I— went through the awkward and sometimes painful and humbling process of settling into immigrant American life, she managed to create in our messy little house full of books and laundry and located in some banal suburban neighborhood, our own world where nothing is mysterious and everything is communal. Instead of waking up in the morning to artifacts of her, she would be there, with a pot of *champorado* on the stove and giggling on the phone with one of her friends, still beautiful, but this time real.

As I read and reread her stories—narratives of our lives, memories of her childhood, tales from the revolution, musings of age, experience and lessons almost learned—I recognize in her interpretations and emphases, the shape of her thoughts, a belief system which in my adolescence seemed haphazard and accidental, but now, after having dabbled in my own adulthood, seems brilliant in its flawed humanity. Through her and the stories she chose to tell, I learned to look for the beauty in imperfection, glean strength from pain and sadness, and find happiness in both the quotidian and the extraordinary. She shaped our world with her words. From what seemed like an endless succession of frustrations and small defeats as we begrudgingly trudged down the path of assimilation, she created neither disillusionment nor resentment, but taught us instead to laugh in the face of inconvenience, welcome the challenges and appreciate the absurdities.

When she started writing the column for *Filipinas* I was disconcerted by her words, words I had known to only speak of politics and the world outside ours, had suddenly turned inward and I was surprised to see my *kapatid* and I factoring into her thoughts and stories, and by the ways that the events which occurred in our lives fed her writing. Rather than remnants and shadows of my mother, her words were mirrors from which I could see life through her eyes, and the view, rather than staring off into the distance and over our shoulders, was actually looking at us. I would wait anxiously every month for her column to appear in the magazine, eager to see what she saw of our life.

In "Love, Patience, and Renewal," she credits me, somewhat unflatteringly, with teaching her patience as she struggled to understand an unaffectionate baby and the headstrong child I became, who fought so fiercely even at the age of four that—at least for a few minutes—she found it a reasonable solution to lock me out of the house. Being my father's child (he paints nearly an opposite picture of me), the teenage years in America without him only exacerbated my tense relationship with my mother.

I moved across the country when I was eighteen, and time and distance have been kind enough to offer us another perspective. While my mother laments in her article the difficulties of raising a child so different from her, the years have shown that those differences were actually similarities. In one of those inevitable conversations with an old friend he declared that I am just like my mother, but rather than vehemently denying this accusation, I recalled her strength as well as the stories of her, legends of bravery and tenacity, most of which she is too humble to tell of herself, and hoped that one day it would be true.

This strength, however, was always balanced with a gleeful girlishness which I discovered, much to my own dismay, when in a trip to the Philippines I uncovered her teenage diary. In a frenzied hand she recounted the minutest details of her interactions with some boy, peppered with declarations of love, only to be replaced by another in a few pages. I'd always imagined my mother to be immune to the foolishness elicited by boys. When I found a stack of 8x10 prints, beautiful close-ups of her face, and asked who's taken them, she flippantly replied that she didn't know. Some earnest admirer had taken them in the cafeteria with a zoom lens but he never overcame his intimidation and had a mutual acquaintance give her the copies. Aloof as she was toward those who didn't interest her, immune she wasn't as she recounts fleeting crushes, dashed hopes, the lingering ego boosts from the otherwise forgettable, as well as the loves lost but never-ending.

As much as she wrote about our life, the stories of the shared experiences of the immigrant, straddling two countries—one present and in flux, the other in memory and nostalgia—speak to me most deeply. In "Summers of Love," she recounts the times when her eccentric aunts from Carcar, Cebu would descend upon the house to cook up a storm, with everything from the *ulam* to the cakes dutifully incorporating freshly extracted lard, the food as delicious as the gossip. Most of the aunts had passed away by the time I was born, but the story greased the wheels of my own memories: the town drunk who roasted the most impossibly tasty *lechon* and preferred to be paid in gin, my informal surveys during fiesta—conducted to the point of extreme discomfort—of which household made the best *paksiw* out of the leftovers, and the days I spent gorging on the incomparable fruits of the tropics: *mangosteen, atis, siniguelas, aratilis, chico, lanzones, manga,* until my belly ached and my soul was satisfied, knowing that I would have to return to the endless cycle of the perfect and perfectly boring fruits of the West, the apples, oranges, pears and the occasional berry, that on my bad days symbolize everything America lacked. Stories of playing in the rain, that warm tropical rain with droplets as big as your head, times when propriety was discarded and the freedom complete—at least for an hour—before you ducked back into the house, elated, with finger tips wrinkled, must be and certainly ought to be universal to the immigrant.

Over the years I have heard and read the reactions of many people to my mother's writing, ranging from amused to empathic, and even emotional. A successful tale isn't a mere retelling of an anecdote, but speaks to the readers' own experiences, resonating in different ways to the shape of their own lives. As you read these stories of our family's immigrant mishaps, the romance of the revolution, her personal tales of trials and victories, I hope, first, that you are delighted, but most of all that you see some reflection of your own memories, trials and triumphs.

Aurora Angela "Jaja" Nemenzo Almendral
New York City, June 2006

Acknowledgments

IT TOOK OVER THREE YEARS AND ALMOST A VILLAGE TO COME OUT WITH THIS book. Hindered by the demands of living in America and my natural inclination for procrastination, I needed to be prodded, nagged, shamed and threatened (well, almost) before I actually buckled down to work.

With a lot of love and gratitude, I'd like to acknowledge those without whose active support this book wouldn't have been possible:

Mona Lisa Yuchengco, founder and former publisher of *Filipinas* Magazine, who trusted me with a regular column from which most of these pieces come;

Rene Ciria Cruz, former editor-in-chief, now contributing editor of *Filipinas*, for his valuable edits and the beautiful titles he gave my columns;

Paulynn Sicam, my editor for this book, for her meticulousness, her patience and her friendship, which made her understand the complicated sentiments I expressed in each piece;

Jojo de Jesus, for never wavering in his belief that I can do it, despite my recalcitrance, and for the constancy of his encouragement;

Carlo, Jaja and Maia, my beloved children who are the main characters of this book, who had to live through all the drama that fed into my writing; Jaja especially for writing such a beautiful foreword that I still couldn't read without stopping to wipe my tears;

Ceres Doyo and Sheila Coronel, for coming up with the book's title;

Irwin Ver, who often had to calm me down and take over the technical tasks when Microsoft Word became too intimidating;

Bumper de Jesus, for the cover design;

Margie Holmes, for not allowing me to say no to publishing this book;

Marites Vitug, Sylvia Mayuga, Ben Pimentel, Bernardo Bernardo, Ray de Guzman, Sonny Alforque, Cristina Pastor, Neni Sta. Romana Cruz and Margie Holmes, for putting in a good word;

Karina Bolasco, for believing in me and the market potential of my essays, and for granting me the help of her marvelous staff.

From the depth of my soul, I thank you all, my immortal friends.

Contents

Foreword by Jaja Nemenzo Almendral   v

Acknowledgments   xi

ASSIMILATION ANGST

Citizen Cain   2

Why We Came   5

What We're Doing Right   9

Assimilation Angst   12

The Terror of It All   15

The Aftermath   18

Balikbayan Blues   21

Third World Guilt   24

Homeward Bound?   27

Should I Stay or Should I Go?   31

Tips for Newcomers   33

THE MOMMY TRACK

Love, Patience, and Renewal   38

The Big Night   42

From Beethoven to the Beatles   45

Letting Go   48

Paternal Instincts   51

Empty Nesting   54

On the Road   57

Call of the Wild   60
Grandparental Moments   63
Taboo or Not Taboo   66

FRIENDS AND LOVERS

Karma Chameleon   70
Take Back the Light   73
Some Never Learn   76
We've Got Mail   81
Romantic Fugue   84
Grieving   87
Basking in the Afterglow   90
To a Dying Friend   93
Karaokay!   96
Girlfriends   99

THE PHILIPPINES IS IN THE HEART

Rainy Days and Fun Days   104
Infidelity   107
May, Come She Will   110
Victual Reality   113
Remembering Cebu in California   116
Savoring Sagada   119
Summers of Love   122
Terms of Endearment   125

MIDDLE-AGE SPREAD

Let's Get Physical 130
The Golden Rules 133
Intimations of Mortality 137
Second Chances 140
The Rhythm of the Dance 143

POLITICS IS PERSONAL

September Memories 148
Paradigm Shift 152
A Heroic August 155
Pain and Remembrance 158
EDSA Is a Terrible Thing to Waste 161
The Other Side of EDSA 164
The End of Her World 168
Secrets and Lies 171
Through Dark Glasses, Brightly 175

assimilation
angst

Citizen Cain

Jewelry was freezing on people's skins in the Midwest, rains were ravaging the East Coast, and floods were threatening the South when I raised my right hand and pledged allegiance to the constitution and the flag of the United States of America.

Though it was a regular foggy and placid winter day in San Francisco, I was feeling the turbulence of the snowstorm, the rains, and the floods inside me, weighing my spirits down even as I tried to be blasé about the almost chaotic ceremony.

"Congratulations, you are now citizens of this great country..." the speaker's voice boomed. Pandemonium broke out as the two thousand recipients of the honor and their families clapped and whooped and hugged and cried. "Now I can petition for my parents," the Chinese woman beside me declared through her tears. As Maia, my little girl, yelled "group hug," someone reminded me of my primary motivation for becoming a U.S. citizen: I'm a voter now! Somehow the realization was not as earth-shaking as I thought it would be.

Nothing will change, this is just a piece of paper. This was my mantra as I went through the whole citizenship process that started a year earlier. When the ceremony finally happened, I feigned detachment and entertained impure thoughts so that I didn't have to listen to the platitudes that the speakers were heaping on us. When we were asked to stand up, raise our right hand, and pledge to "renounce" our loyalties to our old country, I felt a giant lump in my throat and I had to struggle not to cry. By the time they sang the national anthem, they had already lost me.

"Don't forget to register to vote!" the voice boomed again and the new citizens, eager to show their patriotism and their obedience, grabbed voter registration forms. "What's a Republican and what's a Democrat?" somebody asked. "The President is a Democrat and Congress is Republican," somebody answered. A collective "oh" rippled through the crowd as the difference hit them quite pointedly. Just a few days ago, the media reported that some members of Congress were considering taking away the right of immigrants to bring their extended families to the United States. Everyone knew what that meant as we signed up as duly recognized voters of the most successful democracy in the world.

I held my Maia's hand tight as we pushed our way through the crowd. "That was so exciting, Mama!" Maia enthused. She was already planning her presentation in class the next day on how her Mama became an American.

At the restaurant where we celebrated, I gulped down the iced tea, hoping that the constriction in my throat would go away. It didn't, but my emotions were no longer as raw. *Nothing will change, this is just a piece of paper.*

Like many of my friends, my decision to switch citizenship was a pragmatic one. I wanted to be part of the political process and have a say in the future of my children in the country where I live. I wanted us to travel anywhere without being harassed by immigration authorities. Most of all I wanted a clean, uncomplicated divorce and to be beyond the reach of Philippine laws which would allow my ex-husband a share of my estate, in the event of my death.

It has been more than a year since that day I nursed the lump in my throat till sundown and I signed away my Filipino citizenship. I still have not memorized the Pledge of Allegiance or the U.S. National Anthem but I can still sing "Lupang Hinirang" by heart. I have voted and ranted against government, taxes, and crime, like regular Americans do. Our passports remain locked up in a safe, as crisp and clean as the day we got them. Sure, we can travel anywhere now but we just can't afford it.

Has anything changed? Not the shape of my nose, the color of my skin, my food tastes or my accent. When I'm with a Caucasian, some salesclerks still talk to him, like I'm not there, even if I'm the one asking the question. When I walk down the street, nobody will mistake me for an American.

There are days when the possibility of going home for good strikes me as an extremely attractive option. When I was a Filipino citizen, I would banish such thoughts because I was afraid that I'd get stuck once again in the country of my birth. I considered the Philippines as some sort of black hole, not easy to get out of.

This is what being a U.S. citizen is all about to me: It has given me the option of leaving and staying whenever and wherever I want. And it has made me realize that, of all the possible places I would like to spend the next phases of my life in, the Philippines would be at the top of my list.

•*Filipinas Magazine*, August 1997•

Why We Came

In the summer of 2002, fellow columnist Samantha La'O and I were asked to speak at a conference for Filipino American youths and their parents. Samantha voiced the concerns of the young while I tried to explain where Filipino immigrant parents were coming from. Here is part of what I said:

LIKE MOST PARENTS here today, I came to America to carve out a better life. Beyond the money, we wanted a bigger universe where our skills and talents could be honed and used more meaningfully. We were aware coming in that it was not going to be easy "making it" in this new environment. We knew that we had to go through some humbling, like starting out in jobs that were below our experience and qualifications.

But it did not matter; we convinced ourselves that the rewards would be big. We would bring up our children with Filipino values intact. Our children would not have to endure a life of want and uncertainty, they would get a good education and would be set for life. By sheer perseverance and a lot of luck, everything would be hunky-dory, and then we would go home to the Philippines to retire in comfort. The Filipino dream in broad strokes.

But life is never as simple as we want it to be; in fact, it has the habit of throwing some unexpected twists. And one of the many twists that we were not really prepared for—because we never really understood what it meant until we moved here—was this: Our children became Americans.

A part of us considered this our triumph because by growing up Americans, our kids would no longer be subjected to the indignities that we, first-generation immigrants, had to endure to be part of this society. Or so we thought.

But a greater part of us struggled with this new world that our children operated in. This was different; this was strange. The rules and traditions that defined and sheltered us when we were growing up were no longer workable. We twisted and turned, groped and ploded our way through the thicket of our ignorance.

We tried being strict and authoritarian because this was how we were brought up, but it only served to alienate our children. We skirted the edges of permissiveness but it was beyond our comfort level. So we conveyed conflicting messages which only served to confuse our kids more.

Added to this cultural dilemma was the psychological one. Let me cite an example. Remember that first real date of the eldest child? It was not as disturbing as "the first boyfriend" or "the first girlfriend" but it came close, didn't it? Our kids might have asked during this gut-wrenching episode, "Mom, what's the big deal? It's going to be in school and this guy I'm going with is just a friend. Why are you making such an issue of this?"

Well, it was a big issue—to us. Realizing that our kids are almost grown up meant we now had to confront the emotional baggage that we had carried with us through the years and through our many moves. And more often than not, our emotional baggages included a lot of pain and insecurity.

As parents dealing with adolescents, we went through the constant tug and pull between allowing our kids to be kids, to make their own mistakes and protecting them from making too big a mistake or from wasting their time repeating our mistakes. We remembered our rebelliousness and we were afraid our children would be doing what we did in our youth.

These dilemmas reared their ugly heads in various situations with our children, from something as simple as asking them to turn down the music or as emotion-laden as ordering them to keep the bedroom door open when their boyfriends or girlfriends came over.

We grew up in simpler times and in a culture where boundaries were more clearly defined. Our parents made the rules and we were supposed to follow them, no questions asked, even if the prohibitions were ridiculous. But in exchange for these restrictions, we had the advantage of an adolescence free from the pressures of having to earn our own keep.

We were expected to live with our parents until we got married. We went straight to college after high school and our parents paid for our tuitions. When we embarked on our own journeys after graduation, we were still tethered to the safety net of values and traditions that have endured relatively unchanged through generations.

And when we fell in love, it was on the assumption that our first boyfriend or girlfriend would be the one we would marry. Thus we took our time choosing. This was why when our kids had their first boyfriend or girlfriend, it triggered a lot of interrogation and restrictions from us. Our first instinct was to look at this watershed event with caution—Is he or she good in-law material?—forgetting that in this day and age, our kids have a lot of options and are freer to make up their own minds.

When we chose to move to America, in effect, we cut the umbilical cord that linked us to that safety net that had cradled us through our growing-up years. It was a giant leap of faith, something that only the bravest and most determined risk-takers were able to do.

And so we navigated our new world without benefit of operating instructions. Earning a living and setting up a comfortable home for the family—that was the easier part. (Take note that I said easier, not easy.) The more challenging part was raising our children, because there we tread on tricky waters.

We hear our children when they complain about our strictness and what they consider our flawed logic. We know they don't want us to meddle too much in their lives or push them in directions they are not really interested in. We understand how annoying we can get when we insist on our way of doing things. We are aware that laying the guilt trip on them does not really work, and hearing us say "no" too often only drives them to more creative ways of subverting our orders. We know all these yet we continue to do them. Why?

Perhaps part of it is a fear of the unknown. Again, this environment that our kids are living in is strange to us and our primal reaction is to invoke the familiar, so we insist on the ways we are used to, with some modifications. Maybe some of us are afraid that if we loosen our grip on our children, they will be swallowed up by the bigger society, whose values we may not share. We've lived long enough to know about the big bad wolves out there that we want to protect them from.

Okay, admittedly, we often overdo it. We forget that it's them, not us, who have to define their roles among their peers and in the broader society they have to be a part of. But I hope our kids realize this: We may cloak ourselves with the traditions and values that have worked well for us but which now clash with their realities. But at the very core of our being, there is only one thing that keeps us going, and that's our unconditional love for them, our children.

•*Filipinas* Magazine, April 2003•

What We're Doing Right

WE FILIPINOS IN AMERICA have perplexed analysts because, as a demographic group, we have the lowest poverty rate. The *San Francisco Examiner*, which broke this story, wrote: "Filipinos have a household poverty rate so shockingly low, it begs the question, 'what are they doing right?'"

We know the answer to that one: We struggle with all that is in us to make it in this country. We hold multiple jobs, scrimp and save on everything except food, buy lotto tickets religiously, pray fervently, and never pass up a chance to reduce our bills. In many cases, the latter means taking in another person—preferably someone gainfully employed —to live with us for a negotiated fee. No matter if the house is small and there are not enough bathrooms; we never whined about being cramped back home, did we? At least in America we are assured of the convenience of running water and electricity all the time.

Of course there will inevitably come a *bagong salta,* a newly arrived cousin of a friend of a friend who will need a place to stay in while looking for a job. So we willingly accommodate this person—we have been, after all, in the same boat ourselves and we are just giving back the graces that we have received—until such time s/he is able to save enough to move out to his/her own place and then this person likewise does the same for newbies. The cycle continues.

I have never encountered a homeless Filipino although I am pretty sure there are a few somewhere. And I'm also pretty sure that they are homeless essentially by choice because it takes so little for a *kababayan* to feed and house someone especially if s/he is related, however flimsily, to him/her. And for Filipinos everywhere, three degrees of separation is often too much; all we do is ask the all-important first question: *taga saan ka sa atin?* Where are you from back home? And almost always we are able to trace some kind of relationship between his/her lineage and ours.

Tess Uriza Holthe, the author of *When Elephants Dance*, was able to weave an entire novel out of the stories told her by her family and by the many guests that passed through her home. Like most of us who grew up Filipino, she did not find it unusual that there were people other than her immediate family staying with her. The parade of new faces was not deemed an intrusion of privacy but rather a rich source of new stories.

One of the losses I felt when my children and I moved to America was the absence of our own little community, like we had back home where friends and extended family freely came and visited us whenever they were in our area, and did not think twice about dining with us or staying the night. No appointments had to be set, no apologies about not having enough beds, no bickering over bathroom time. In our small house in Quezon City, we only had one bathroom that we shared with our visitors, our maids, and often even our maids' friends who also felt free to stay for days or weeks when they were between jobs.

The inconveniences that we couldn't seem to live with anymore here in America, were no big deal then. The important thing was that we opened our homes to friends and relations, especially to those who needed food and shelter. We were, I guess, the epitome of Filipino hospitality, the unique national trait that had been alternately praised and dissed (author's note: too colloquial? Suggestions: disparaged, assailed, denounced, condemned, lambasted, reviled) by historians and sociologists.

I am perhaps more used to cramped living than the usual middle-class Filipino because I grew up in a university campus. This meant that my parents, like most other university employees living on site, took in boarders. In our case, we always had at least three women sharing the big bedroom in our *sawali* cottage, and we moved our beds to new positions every month to make our living spaces more interesting. The issue of privacy was never a major consideration, especially because our close friends would come over and hang out between classes so there was always a small party going on.

When I listen to my children complain about how small their individual rooms are and grumble over having to share a bathroom, I cannot help but weigh the gains and losses our moving here has brought us. On the one hand, each of us have found our voice and sense of self; on the other, we no longer have the sense of intimate community that sustained us through the hardships that we encountered back home.

There was a World Bank report some years back that stated that among Asians, Filipinos are the happiest. Seen against the backdrop of dirty politics, economic difficulties, and natural disasters, even Filipinos were surprised by the results of the study. But what we tend to forget is that deep within our collective souls, we Filipinos have figured out the essence of true happiness: Our *pakikipag-kapwa,* our interconnectedness with one another that motivates us to form our little communities.

So the next time we feel like pulling a *kababayan* down, let us take a minute to revive our inner Filipino, the little voice within that reminds us that we are all in this together and that our strength lies in our ability to help each other. This, not our income, is what makes our poverty rate here in America so shockingly low. This is what we are doing right.

•*Filipinas* Magazine, July 2002•

Assimilation Angst

WE ARE SETTLED. We are no longer ignorant and wide-eyed about the ways and wonders of America. Our stay in this country has become permanent; we now "come home" to the United States and "visit" the Philippines. This place we are in is not just a transition between youth and old age. We have grown roots that dig deep into the ground, pushed firmly in place by our debts and mortgages, our changed manners and our children who see themselves as more American than Filipino. Our tastes have been redefined by a consciousness of healthy living, our accents affected by the twang of American English. Even our humor has changed.

We spend our weekends watching sports. We are conversant about Democrats and Republicans, of the right to choose versus the right to life, and we laugh at jokes about the NYPD and LAPD, about the rednecks in Kentucky and the yuppies in Washington state. We know what DWB means, and are rightfully appalled that it is happening in this land of the free, but we try to banish this indignation from our comfortable lives.

We have become Americans, maybe not like apple pie, but close enough to make us root for this country in war or in competition. We have sworn allegiance to the American Constitution and gotten over our renunciation of our former citizenship. For the most part, we declare ourselves happy.

But...

Deep in our souls, we know how fragile this carefully crafted life is. Though we try to be as loyal to this country as is expected of those who are reaping a portion of its bounties, we, first-generation immigrants, cannot deny to ourselves that our instincts will always be Filipino.

When American troops are sent for a military operation abroad, we automatically scan the faces for those of Filipino ethnicity. Surfing the TV channels, we always stop at one showing a Filipino face. And though there are enough of our *kababayans* around to make us blasé about their presence everywhere we go, hearing one of our dialects spoken always triggers a smile, even if our American timetable may not allow us to stop and chat.

We laugh out loud at the list of one hundred telltale signs of being Filipino that is making the rounds on the Internet because we have gotten over most of them (no more wooden spoons on our walls, no "man-in-a-barrel" décor, the Last Supper has been replaced by a china cabinet and a painting) but, just between us, we know that some items on the list still apply. Always will, even if we have learned to disguise our "ethnic" ways better.

I have been pondering these thoughts lately because, as I write this piece, the Philippine government is conducting intense military operations in Jolo to wipe out the Abu Sayyaf hostage-takers while trying to rescue the hostages, one of whom is an American from the city right next to where I live. Just like most Filipinos in America who have imbibed the parochial consciousness that prevails in this country, I was not paying too much attention to the "Muslim problem" that had dominated the conversations in Manila for months. But when the bombing started, a wave of overlapping emotions swept through me, triggering an e-mail frenzy to various friends—journalists, military officers, relatives. Gruesome images of the costs of war would wake me up at night. Criticisms by some Americans about the competence of the Philippine military and the righteousness of the decision to bomb upset me even if, in less emotional moments, I would agree with them.

When I became an American citizen some years ago, somebody asked me: if ever the U.S. goes to war against the Philippines, whose side will I take? Thank goodness the possibility of my having to confront the issue is nil, at least in my lifetime, because my answer is: I really don't know. Would I go with my basic instinct or my objective assessment?

Eugene, my childhood buddy, who greets me online each morning from his office a time zone away, is now preparing for his first visit to the Philippines in more than two decades. He has never felt compelled to "go home" before, not when he was starting a career, raising a family, paying off his mortgage, doing all the things that occupy our days here. Also, his entire family has moved to the United States so there is really no one to go home to.

But now, when his children are grown and life has become less frenzied, Eugene can no longer resist the pull of his Filipino-ness. After burying for a long time his memories of things that made him happy— "barbecued chicken at Aristocrat after a party that ends at 3 a.m.; *asadong bituka* (roasted chitlins) at Hong Ning; *lechon* (roast pig) at Mang Tomas; real mangoes, not the Mexican mangoes that we get here; *latundan* bananas, not the tasteless ones from Dole"—he is allowing them free rein in his consciousness. And he has not been the same since.

He bought himself a plane ticket for December.

"We're growing old," he tells me (as if I needed reminding), "and I tend to be more romantic. I want to stop and smell the [Philippine] flowers. Might be my last…"

Those of us who've been on multiple *balikbayan* visits know only too well what Eugene is trying to work out in his (Americanized) mind: that no matter how long it takes, our life journey never fails to bring us back to where we come from. And we are all the richer for it.

•*Filipinas* Magazine, November 2000•

The Terror of It All

I WAS AWAKENED this morning by Maia, my thirteen-year-old daughter, who ran into my room screaming, "Mama, the World Trade Center tower collapsed!" I bolted out of bed and ran downstairs to turn the TV on. What I saw was a scene so totally insane: Smoke billowing out of one of the WTC towers then a plane crashing into the other one. I literally froze in my seat—from the shock, the unspeakable horror, from disbelief. The reports came fast and furious: the Pentagon had been hit, a car bomb exploded in Washington D.C., flights all over the country were cancelled, airports closed, government buildings and San Francisco landmarks evacuated.

I ran upstairs to wake up Jaja, my older daughter, who has lived in New York for the past two years but has decided to study in San Francisco for the semester. "The World Trade Center has been bombed," I said. She picked up her glasses and ran downstairs yelling, "No, no" with her every step. She was almost hysterical as we watched the two New York landmarks collapse to rubble. For Jaja, the pain was like losing something personal. From her dorm, she had a view of the twin towers from her window. She had found her way through the streets of Lower Manhattan and Greenwich Village by situating herself in relation to the towers.

An American friend who, like most Americans born after World War II, had not experienced any terror this close to home, was glued to his TV set. "I just feel so personally assaulted," he confessed. "It feels like I'm being hit in the chest by an unknown force."

I called Maia's school to find out if classes have been suspended. "No," the attendance officer declared, her voice betraying her fear. "But if you want to keep your child home, we will understand." Maia squeezed beside me on the recliner. We were all mesmerized and speechless at the scenes unfolding before us.

We who live in the United States have been quite smug about the threat of terrorism. Sure, we've heard the warnings and we are aware that as the world's only remaining superpower, the country is definitely a target. But the constant rhetoric we've also heard about how the country's military and intelligence capabilities are unparalleled, gave us a sense of security that made us pooh-pooh the threats as mere saber rattling by the nation's enemies—all bark, no bite.

Until today, when we actually saw what we thought were impenetrable shrines crumble to oblivion. A chill so palpable I could almost touch it, ran through my spine as I went from telephone to TV to computer, trying to contact friends in New York ("all circuits are busy," a recorded voice declared). In San Francisco, all schools and many offices were closed. The three airports have been evacuated. Many malls have decided to shut down completely. I got a call from my boss, who was making sure everyone was accounted for.

Our carefully crafted and comfortable lives have been shattered by these terrorist acts that were so well coordinated and sophisticated, one couldn't help but be impressed despite the rage that was consuming us. Government officials were saying that this was the beginning of a very different era in America, that life as we knew it would never be the same again.

A fear begins to gnaw at me. The war mongers in Washington may assume a bunker mentality and curtail some of the civil liberties that we have been taking for granted. A hawkish legislator has already declared that the priority now is defense, not education. Another has warned that we should be ready to give up some of the conveniences we are used to. Already there are reports of enraged fanatics targeting people whose only sin is to look Middle Eastern. This kind of irrational bigotry strikes fear in non-whites like us.

I called Carlo in San Diego, the site of one of the U.S. Navy's biggest installations and one of the borders to Mexico which has been declared closed. "Nothing is moving here, Mom," he said. "Everyone has been told to go home and stay home."

Except for the media, the entire country seems to have shut down, the people retreating to the bomb shelters in their mind.

It is almost midnight now, the end of a day of unspeakable horror. I cannot sleep. I have a nagging headache. I decide to scrub the kitchen, do the laundry, mop the floor, water the plants, anything to keep the images of the day from slamming back into my consciousness.

I await another day in America knowing full well that everything has changed. The U.S. mainland is vulnerable after all. In just a matter of minutes, the greatest power in the world has been reduced to just another nation dogged by instability and uncertainty. May God grant us the good sense to be humbled by all these and the strength to rise up and rebuild the America we have always known: strong, magnanimous, and able to celebrate with the rest of the world our common humanity.

•*Newsbreak*, September 2001•

The Aftermath

As I DROVE into the parking lot of the mile-long walking trail at the San Leandro Marina yesterday, I was greeted by the sight of hundreds of schoolchildren, each with plastic gloves and green recycling bags, picking up litter in the park and shoreline. It was an emotional moment for me—in this week of highly charged moments—watching the children do their task, hearing their lively chatter, oblivious (at least for that hour) of the tragedy that had befallen the nation and the war clouds hovering in the horizon.

This is my America, I thought, a land of peace and responsibility, where everyone pulls together to do what has to be done, whether in searching for survivors in the rubble of the World Trade Center and the Pentagon, or in making our immediate environment cleaner. Juxtaposed with the horror that we had all witnessed in the days just past are images and tales of so much goodness, unity, and selflessness.

I saw my America in the words of that farmer who was asked on TV what he was praying for and quickly, without hesitation, he said he was praying for the souls of those who perished in the terrorist attacks and their families. "Are you praying for yourself, too?" he was asked. "I don't have problems," this man who faces a difficult road ahead replied, "those are the people with problems."

My America is evident in the people who stand in line in blood banks for hours, in the exhausted firefighters in New York who were energized after pulling out five people who were alive after being buried for two days in the rubble, among the seniors in the grocery stores dropping money in collection boxes, in the sad faces of students in Berkeley listening to a poet speak of the ascendance of love and justice over blind revenge and hatred.

I admit that I'm frantically ferreting out these instances of a united America amidst the increasing shrillness of the rhetoric of war that is now dominating the airwaves. I cling to these stories and images because deep inside me I am scared and saddened by an America going berserk in its rage and its single-minded quest for punishing the guilty.

Just as I grieve for the missing and the dead in New York, I lament the senseless deaths of two Arab Americans in Texas, lynched by lunatics who think that the American flag and the patriotic slogans that they have wrapped themselves with have given them the right to set free their bigotry and their hatred.

I cry as I listen to this beautiful third-generation Arab American woman who can no longer take her two small children to the park for fear that they will be harmed by people who judge them by their looks. "My parents were born here, I was born here, my children were born here—how much more American do I have to be?" she asks.

I ask my thirteen-year-old daughter Maia how she feels now that the terrorist attacks seem to have subsided. "Scared," she answers. Not so much because of the possibility of another attack but because the president talks so much about going to war, she explains. Without any prodding from me, Maia—and many American children—understands instinctively that war will hurt many innocent people just as much or even more than Americans are hurting now. "And nobody should get hurt anymore," she adds.

But that is not the mood of the hour in this America still reeling from the unspeakable terror that has reached its shores. Everywhere you look there are American flags waving, and even rock stations are playing patriotic songs. Which is quite a change because democratic America has always prided in the First Amendment, the freedom to speak out, and

19

most of the time people speak out against the government. But scratch the surface of these collective proclamations of love for country and you'll find a thirst for the blood of others as retribution for Black Tuesday.

We have a cheerleader president who mouths platitudes when he should be explaining the context of this tragedy in terms of history and the role of America in the international community; a president who leaves the discussion of substantial issues to his cabinet (come to think of it, this is actually a good thing).

Reserve troops have been called to active duty, the sabers are rattling in Washington and the dogs of war are about to be unleashed. Be ready for a long and costly conflict, we are told over and over, as if the constant repetition will blunt the fear of someday seeing the young men of this country sent to slaughter in pursuit of an elusive enemy.

I am tempted to bury my head in the sand and just pray that I am wrong about this other America. But I take heart from the many e-mail messages that are circulating from people all over the world suggesting caution and providing information about the real state of the Afghan people and the Pakistanis, who are about to bear the brunt of American military power.

I write my friends whose opinions I regard highly and am heartened that they too feel the same way about the horror of the impending war. Already groups of concerned citizens are banding together to advocate peace, but cautiously, lest they trip the war fuses of the majority who support massive retaliation.

There are long, dark days ahead for a changed America and I can only pray that the slivers of light that I see peeking through the anger and despair will eventually overpower the gloom.

•*Newsbreak*, September 2001•

Balikbayan Blues

I'M IN PANIC MODE. Right now my living room is strewn with stuff that I have collected from the many sales of the past seven months, ever since I scheduled another *balikbayan* visit. And like a typical Pinoy getting ready to go back to the homeland, I alternate between excitement and expectation, dread and fatigue.

I have not been sleeping well the past week. I am constantly making lists that range from things-to-do-before-we-leave to things-to-buy-there-to-bring-here. Then there's the gift list, possible-places-to-visit list, must-buys-from-the-places-we-visit list, books-to-bring list, snacks-to-eat-on-the-plane list, tokens to hand out if the Customs people in Manila give us a hard time—god, the stress can be overwhelming.

Anyone who suggests that a *balikbayan* visit is easy does not understand the preparation it entails. Unless you are one of the lucky souls who go home regularly on business, a visit takes a lot of planning. The moment a date for departure is set, one gets into a *balikbayan* frame of mind, which means being always on the lookout for stuff to bring home. It can also take a lot of soul-searching, which is almost like therapy—where you have to look deep inside yourself and think about who you really care for and how much. Who gets a good *pasalubong* and who doesn't. Who gets a gift that will be bought in the Duty Free Shop in Manila and who doesn't get any gift at all.

It is easy to obsess about the quality and the quantity of one's gifts because it comes naturally to us Pinoys to hand out *pasalubong* like they come from a bottomless well. This innate generosity never fails to perplex a non-Filipino. Years ago, when a group of Filipino women journalists (myself included) went to China for a "friendship visit," an American woman who had been there suggested that each of us bring five inexpensive token gifts to hand to our guides at the end of the tour. Which we did, but we liked our guides so much that by the third day of the two-week visit, we had nothing left to give. For our American friend, gifts are rewards for time well-spent; to us, they are expressions of affection and appreciation. And of kinship.

Some sour-graping Filipino I know once said that *balikbayans* bring a lot of stuff home to show off. The I've-done-better-than-you syndrome. Sure there are people who fall under this category but for the most part, I think *balikbayans* are motivated mainly by the desire to share the bounties they have received. Why do we fill every inch of a 20-by-20-inch box with goodies? Because we can.

Buying gifts, however, is the easy part of the *balikbayan's* quest. It is the packing that requires skill and contemplation. One has to weigh the desire to please over the need to stick to the 70-pound limit. "They'll be deliriously happy if I bring a microwave oven but that's too heavy so I have to scale down to a blender. But a blender takes up too much space and look at all the other stuff I have to fit in the box, so I will have to settle for a cookbook and bags of chocolate. But if I give this person a bag, do I have enough to give to others? Do I have to buy some more? Will they fit in the box? Will the box be too heavy that I have to take out some stuff, in which case, I won't have anything to hand to the others?" The rules of international travel are simply too unfriendly to Pinoys.

At airports, you know exactly which flights are going to Manila by the *balikbayan* boxes lined up before the check-in counters. No other nationality even comes close. Flights to El Salvador will have people carrying large plastic *bayongs* but not in the same scale as our boxes. Those going to Europe or to other Asian countries will have the occasional golf bags or surfboards but never the 20-by-20-inch white boxes. What is wrong with those people? And what is right with us?

Years ago, an old man from the Mountain Province explained to me his tribe's concept of wealth. A person's wealth is not measured by how much he has acquired, he said, it is measured by how much he can give away. I try to keep this nugget of wisdom in mind whenever I am confronted by the overpowering temptations of the consumer culture. It has stopped me from spending too much and acquiring things that end up as dust-traps on my shelves.

But, of course, when it's time for a *balikbayan* visit, all that wisdom goes out the window.

•*Filipinas* Magazine, April 2000•

Third World Guilt

I USED TO CRINGE whenever I'd hear someone utter the cliché, "You can take the Filipino out of the Philippines but you can't take the Philippines out of the Filipino." Here comes the inevitable marketing pitch, I would tell myself, and then I would let my mind go blank, letting the pitch whoosh by me without so much as a dent in my consciousness.

But now that I have grown older and more forgiving of pitch makers and politicians, I have come to appreciate the truth in that cliché. Like most first-generation immigrants who moved to this country as adults, there are certain things that we just cannot shake off or even dilute. And I am not talking about accents, way of dressing, or food tastes.

One of the most tenacious is what I facetiously call "Third World guilt," an attitude that can be both endearing and repulsive. It was Third World guilt that made me grumble to my children, each time they picked on their food or left a lot uneaten, that they were too spoiled and wasteful, that they should not forget the millions of children in—take your pick—Manila, India, Afghanistan, who do not have anything to eat. They would roll their eyes and attempt to humor me by finishing off as much as they could, until they could not take anymore and then it was up to me to eat whatever was left on their plates.

Until one day, one of them, in mock earnestness, suggested that I send the leftovers to the starving children instead because they were getting sick of my guilt tripping and I was getting fat from the extra food intake. I stopped my nagging then, at least on the issue of their eating habits.

It did not stop me, however, from saving leftovers, even if I knew we would never eat them again. How I wish we had a dog or a pig to pass them on to, I would say, remembering our dogs back home and the scrawny little boy who used to go around the neighborhood gathering *kanin-baboy*, pig food. (I conveniently forgot that in this country, where pets are better cared for than people, feeding your dog scraps from the kitchen instead of scientifically formulated dog food could be considered scandalous, or even somewhat criminal.) I would let these leftovers decay into science experiments in the refrigerator before throwing them out. Sure it was gross but better than to be haunted by the faces of starving children.

This same congenital guilt made me set aside a box where I would stash stuff that I intended to send to the Philippines. In it I would put useless little knickknacks such as freebies at marketing events or when I donate money to a charity; stuffed toys that I won in amusement parks; items I would buy in garage sales and discount stores but couldn't find any use or space for; clothes that were still good but the kids have outgrown; leftover Halloween candies; shoes I could not wear because they pinched in the wrong places; Christmas decorations that I bought at seventy-five percent off; books I got on sale but would not be reading again; and a big pile of magazines that I couldn't bear to throw away. I wanted to donate them to the public library in my father's rural hometown.

Never mind that my family back home actually had no use for most of these stuff, that they had actually hinted that they found it quite insulting to be the recipient of our discards, no matter how well-intentioned the gesture was. Just give them all away, I would instruct. I assumed everyone would be grateful for the largesse from good ol' US of A, the big PX in the sky. But when I went home one year, I was surprised to see a pile of things that I had sent still sitting in their boxes, unwanted. Worse, I saw better versions of some of the stuff in stores in Manila, at prices more attractive than what I paid for them in the Bay Area. My First World magnanimity was dashed by Third World ingenuity.

Am I the only one afflicted by this guilt/generosity syndrome? I suspect there are many of us who feel the same way. The door-to-door forwarders are thriving and each time a Philippine Airlines flight leaves the United States for home, it is filled to the rafters with *balikbayan* boxes. And that is a good thing. I think our propensity for gift giving and sharing our blessings with our relatives back home is a trait we should always be proud of.

In moments of introspection, however, I can't help but feel that this generosity can be overdone, that there is a thin line separating thoughtfulness from insensitivity, genuine caring from bragging. It was a humbling experience for me, seeing that pile of unwanted stuff in my sister's house, because I realized that gifts carelessly given are worse than not giving anything at all.

I know better now. Whenever I get the chance to send something home, I ask each one of my family for a list of things they need or want from here that are not available there. And when I do my annual assessment of stuff to be given away, I end up hauling a bigger stash to the local charities that collect them instead of dumping them all into *balikbayan* boxes. After all, turtleneck sweaters and winter boots are not coveted items in our homeland. And magazines that talk about "how to drive men crazy in bed" and "how to lose weight in twenty days" will do nothing to improve the life of a young mother who can hardly feed her family a full meal each day.

•*Filipinas* Magazine, October 2002•

Homeward Bound?

Always keep Ithaca in your mind.
To arrive there is your ultimate goal.
But do not hurry the voyage at all.
It is better to let it last for many years,
And to anchor at the island when you are old,
Rich with all you have gained on the way,
Not expecting that Ithaca will offer you riches.

Ithaca has given you the beautiful voyage
Without her you would have never set out on the road.
– "Ithaca" by Constantine Cavafy (1911)

WITH THE WORLD ECONOMY in the dumps and layoffs becoming part of the daily news, many Filipino immigrants, especially those close to retirement, are thinking of going home to the Philippines. The magnets are many: Retirement dollars go a longer way in our home country, the comfort of being with the extended family and on familiar grounds, the loneliness of growing old in America, among them. The turn-offs are just as many, of course, depending on one's tolerance and cynicism levels.

I'm not close enough to retirement age—both financially and chronologically—to seriously consider moving back, yet that option, which has always been in my mind, is becoming more and more attractive as I struggle through a displacement. Life in America, as we working stiffs who toil from paycheck to paycheck know, is not always the bed of roses that we imagine it to be; most of the time it is a mixed bag of hard labor, meager rewards, and numbing detachment from the rest of the real world.

Deciding to pack up and return to where one started from is a very involved, often long, drawn-out process. It is just as much a psychological decision as it is a practical one. Many times the beacon comes stealthily, like the proverbial thief in the night, hardly recognized at first but eventually growing into a nagging restlessness. We start out by ignoring it, then brushing it aside as foolishness. Many times, we succeed in keeping our restlessness in check, sublimated by all the lures of America—the valuable dollars, the convenience, the cleanliness, and the creature comforts. However, at some point, such lures start losing their luster and homesickness sets in.

We schedule regular *balikbayan* trips and start getting interested again in Philippine events. We actively look for ways to help the folks back home. We look at the offers of real estate deals for condominium properties or provincial retreats, especially those created for people like us who may be returning but will not give up on the many conveniences of our adopted country. Class reunions become big events, old friendships are renewed.

We surprise ourselves when we realize that we are no longer as negative about our homeland's many woes. When the scent of the humid salt air and the sight of our childhood haunts take center stage in our consciousness, the inconveniences somehow recede into the background.

My personal homeward journey is still in its initial stage but I already recognize it as a mindshift that is both disturbing and exhilarating. I think it began when I got in constant touch with my high school classmates, sharing our thoughts about how our lives have been and how we want to grow old. Before I knew it, the lure of home—and everything that it represented—became a fever. I visited three years in a row and enjoyed each one increasingly, putting me back to the psychological place I was in during my first years in the United States: straddling two countries, unable to decide where I really belonged.

I began to feel this hunger in my soul to reconnect with our culture, not just through the usual channels (books, songs, and events) but also by meeting new people with whom I have a shared past. My idea of fun shifted from doing things American to remembering things Filipino and sharing stories with people who were part of the scene when I was there. "It's just so comforting to not have to provide a context to the topic I'm talking about," I told a friend. "I just barge right in and the other person knows where I'm coming from." Funny, even Filipino males became interesting again.

Someone visiting from Manila asked me recently which feels more like home to me—the Philippines or the Bay Area. Five years ago, I would have unequivocally answered the latter but now, I could not answer the question directly. In fact, it triggered some nagging questions in me that I still have not found answers for, since they address certain issues that I thought were long buried in the dustbin of my unconscious.

For those of us who are in the cusp of a life-changing decision (such as where will you live the rest of your life), the appeal of going home may be like the ebb and flow of the tide: one day it is strong, the next day it feels unreal. There are major practical considerations after all, and to turn our backs on a comfortable life here is as much a leap of faith as the one we took coming here. But there is also the adventurer in each of us and, like Odysseus, though we may travel far and wide, we will ultimately find our way back to where we started from, our own Ithaca.

•*Filipinas* Magazine, July 2003•

Should I Stay
or Should I Go?

IF YOU'RE A Filipino expat hooked up to the Internet, you must have been bombarded these past months with e-mail forwards about why people leave the Philippines and why others choose to stay. The intense discussions emanated from the highly publicized decision of Dr. Elmer Jacinto, that chap from Basilan who, after topping the medical board exams, declared that he was moving to the United States to work as a nurse.

Not surprisingly, he was excoriated and praised in equal measure by Filipinos in the Philippines, each of whom must have pondered the issue of leaving and staying at some point in their lives.

The news also triggered a flurry of postings from Filipino students in the United States who are planning to return home after graduation and are immensely proud of it. Filipino overseas workers and other expats joined in the fray, and pretty soon, the decibel level of what was essentially a significant discussion rose exponentially, and a cyberspace "West Side Story," with the leavers on one side and the stayers on the other (each one smug in a holier-than-thou perch), threatened to erupt.

Under the cloak of journalistic curiosity, I read each of these postings thoroughly, maintaining my neutrality (or at least trying to), giving each argument weight, swinging from amusement to amazement at how someone's very personal decision had ballooned into a collective examination of conscience over how we should and how much we love our home country. I switched off only when the rhetoric became too strident to bear and more reasonable voices, such as Patricia Evangelista's (she's the young Filipina who won first place in an international public speaking competition in the United Kingdom), emerged to elevate the cyberdebate to a higher plane.

But the question that Dr. Jacinto's decision posed—should personal goals take precedence over duty to country?—lingered in my consciousness long after the din had subsided, because this was not the first time I, and my generation of Filipinos, have been confronted by the many nuances of the issue.

We asked ourselves when we graduated from college: Should we go for the gold in the United States or should we stay in the Philippines to do our part in seeking social justice for all? When Ferdinand Marcos declared martial law, we again had to ask ourselves: Do we fight or do we succumb? Should we choose a safe and stable *petit bourgeois* life over the romance of revolution? For many, the decision was easy since the choice was clear cut. The Marcos regime, after all, had polarized the country into those who had the power and those who didn't.

But time, altered family circumstances, and maturity have a way of muddling the simplicity of either-or decisions. Many of those who took to the hills and offered their lives to the cause of liberating the masses from "imperialism, fascism, and bureaucrat capitalism" survived and found themselves needing to fend in the broader "legal" society where the options were more varied and the choices much more complex. Those who were working safe, comfortable jobs were confronted with different but equally perplexing questions.

When I decided to move to the United States in 1988, my choices were no longer between personal comfort and love of country. Simply put, I had to leave the Philippines because it was the only way I could survive, and I'm not (just) talking about economics. Even then, I was ambivalent about the morality of my choice. Having been brought up under the mantle of nationalism (my family never considered immigration an option), it took years before I could say unequivocally that I am now an American, without adding, defensively, that I did not abandon the Philippines and I will always be a Filipino in my heart.

Which brings me back to the controversy that Dr. Jacinto's decision triggered. What started out as a to-leave-or-not-to-leave issue eventually morphed into a self-esteem issue ("Doesn't that doctor have any pride?" "Is title and poverty more noble than anonymity and creature comforts?"), and branched out into arguments on the hopelessness or hopefulness of the Philippine situation, and the trade-offs of living in the United States. Valid and worthy discussions, to be sure, but they miss out on the essential reality: In today's world of Internet connectivity, instant messaging, direct flights and satellite communications, geographic boundaries are no longer as formidable as they used to be and one can be as much a Filipino in the Middle East, North America, or Europe, as those who remain in the Philippines.

A top-ranking Philippine educator who had been disapproving of young and highly educated professionals leaving the country, had a paradigm mind shift when he held dialogues with successful Filipinos in the United States, notably Dado Banatao, the Silicon Valley venture capitalist. Banatao and many other Pinoy expats are actively involved in development projects in the Philippines, sharing the expertise and experience they have garnered here with our countrymen in various places in our homeland.

Seeing how these professionals are spending time and resources to help improve the lot of our *kababayans,* the educator came to realize the value of spreading one's professional wings and learning from other countries. China, South Korea, India, and even Vietnam have clearly illustrated that expats are valuable resources, not traitors to one's country of origin.

In this global village we live in, a person's character is not determined by his leaving the country to live and work in another land. It is defined by how he gives back to the community that nurtured him.

•*Filipinas* Magazine, July 2004•

Tips for Newcomers

IT WAS A REGULAR cold and rainy day, I remember very vividly, when my three small children and I stepped out of the customs area of the San Francisco International Airport, into the warm embraces of relatives and finally into the car that took us to our new life as immigrants. Sixteen years this month. More years than each of my children spent in our homeland, and certainly more years than what I originally planned on spending in the United States.

As I try to step back and look at the past sixteen years on hindsight, I discover that our first five years are a blur in my memory. I know we moved house three times and my two older kids advanced from elementary to high school. I know I spent most of my day working in the office and had to do grocery shopping at midnight, after the kids were asleep, the dishes washed, my baby breastfed, and all the necessary chores completed. But I don't remember, or purposely shut out the memory of, how each one of us felt or coped with the uprooting and the adjusting, the strangeness and, yes, the homesickness.

I had leaped from the security of home to an undefined life in a new land, bringing my kids along for the ride. It was the proverbial choice between the devil and the deep blue sea in more ways than one. Was I stupid or was I crazy? Deciding to immigrate (in the midst of my personal crisis, the approval of our visas arrived unexpectedly) was a no-brainer. I didn't bother to be scared about the future. I had to leave, I wanted to leave and nothing was going to stop me. Not even the fact that I was ending my marriage and would have to negotiate my new world alone.

It is not easy being an immigrant, as most of us know only too well. There are hundreds of little things to comprehend, gadgets to conquer, obstacles to overcome. The emotional and mental implications alone are staggering. But somehow we survive; altered for sure in many different ways by the experience, yet ready, if need be, to do it all over again.

So in the spirit of patting each other's back for our successes (whether real or imagined), here are some insights to share with those who will come after us:

1. Bring souvenirs and mementos to get you through the many moments when you will feel like taking the next flight home. Most importantly, come with an open mind unencumbered by your ego. Like a military boot camp, only prettier, life in America will humble you into submission and it will take every ounce of determination on your part not to subsume your identity completely to its wiles.

2. Accept that the rules have changed, literally, and you now have to: develop a stronger stomach for slights (intended and unintended), keep a lid on your tendency to make fun of people of various ethnicities, do household chores and realize that your children have more freedom now to question your demands and pursue their real interests, whether you approve of them or not.

3. It will take time to let go of the Philippines. Until your first *balikbayan* visit, you will always be comparing home to here, and often home will always win out in your mind. It is normal to take five years before you can really say you are now comfortable in your new circumstance. It might take another *balikbayan* visit before you can completely switch off the lights and close the door to your old life.

4. Learn to appreciate little triumphs—getting the dishwasher to work, finding your way out of the freeway, buying a phone card that doesn't cheat you too much, locating the nearest Asian store. Just concentrate on whatever it takes to get you through a day or a night at a time. Looking far into the future is a luxury accorded only those who have "made it" in this country. It's something to look forward to, later.

5. It is so easy to be so comfortable here and thus be numb to the realities of the rest of the world. Life in America is the drug of choice of millions but it can give you a sense of complacency and kill your spirit. You embarked on a great adventure when you moved here; don't abandon the daring and curiosity that came with it. Be always ready to take flight once again, even if you don't really do it. Even if it's only in your mind.

•*Filipinas* Magazine, November 2004•

the mommy track

Love, Patience, and Renewal

IF, AT THE END of my journey, I am asked what I learned from this life, I would unhesitatingly say, from my eldest child who is my only son, I learned to love without measure; from my older daughter, I learned acceptance; and with my youngest daughter, I came to understand the full meaning of resurrection.

I would talk about that time before my first child was even on the horizon, when the twin forces of society and biology conspired to plant in me a deep, unshakable longing to procreate. The pressure started soon after college, when my friends began getting married and having children. At the weddings, baptisms, and children's birthday parties I went to, inevitably, someone would ask when my turn would come.

Then there was my mother. After I lived out my twenty-fourth year, she started discreetly questioning my close friends about my love life. She married at twenty-four, my brother and sister married when they were twenty-four, and there I was, past twenty-four and without a spouse in sight. Though she wouldn't admit it to anyone, I could sense she was worried that nobody would want her daughter.

And then there was me. I really wanted a child. Whether it was due to the ticking of my biological clock or the creeping horror of going through life alone and unloved, the prospect of motherhood appealed to me so much, there was no question of it not actually happening. When I went for my first pregnancy test, and it turned out negative, I was so devastated that my husband had to drive me around the city for hours just so I could take my mind off what I considered was my failure.

I will never forget that when my son was born, a colony of honeybees chose to build a hive in our garden. They didn't stay long—a few days later they moved on—but I always thought it auspicious that it actually happened on my son's first day on earth.

Motherhood was as wonderful as I thought it would be, notwithstanding the interrupted sleep, the worrying over rashes, and my obsession with being the perfect mother. Carlo was so even-tempered, healthy and smart—and I say this with the objectivity of a mother —that I was constantly rhapsodizing about the joys of parenting.

It was when Carlo was about two months old and slept through the night (as opposed to waking up every two hours to nurse) that I realized how vulnerable a parent could be to the possibility of loss. We woke up in the early morning in a panic: Was he still breathing? Did anyone steal him? Our reaction, of course, was not even original. Dr. Spock warned of it in his book, that new parents are often disconcerted (a serious understatement) when, after weeks of waking up often, their baby decides to sleep through the night. He called it a developmental stage; to us, it was a bad joke.

That was also a watershed moment in my own evolution: the unequivocal love that I showered on my child brought with it the gripping fear that he would be taken away from me. The feeling was so strong, it was frightening. Parents know this only too well, the joy-fear that comes with loving another being so completely, your life is unimaginable without him.

With my first foray into motherhood a resounding success, I was ready for the next baby who was born a few hours after the 1980s decade was ushered in by the explosive frenzy that characterizes New Year's Eve in Manila. Though I spent the last weeks of the pregnancy in bed due to extreme exhaustion (I was then working full-time for a business newspaper), giving birth to my daughter was the easiest, most physically satisfying experience I have ever had. And for good reason: I had internalized the teachings of Dr. Lamaze, redefined my concept of pain (toothache is pain, going through labor is not pain but a series of strong sensations that you ride with, not fight against), understood the crucial role of relaxation in the birthing process, and learned to block unpleasant sensations by keeping my mind focused on that which gave me pleasure. (Such skills have since served me well through other intense events in my life.)

Nothing, however—not Lamaze training, not parenting books, not my honed skills as Carlo's mother—prepared me for the reality of Jaja. The first time I held her in my arms and tried to nurse her, I knew immediately that she was a unique individual, quite different from her brother. Carlo would snuggle in my breasts for hours; Jaja, on the other hand, would nurse only until she was full and then she would turn away and refuse to even snuggle.

For someone who naively thought she had this parenting thing figured out, dealing with a colicky baby who had a mind of her own was quite an eye-opener. It was challenging and humbling. Jaja unconsciously tested my ability to love a person who was so unlike me, it sometimes felt that I was nurturing a stranger. It was difficult, but eventually I learned how to be patient.

My relationship with her had always been intense, peppered with shouting matches and tests of will. There were times when I felt so ashamed of myself for not being mature enough—like when she got me so frustrated with her stubbornness (over what, I don't even remember) that I locked her out of the house for a few minutes. Her father was beside himself with disbelief. "You're her mother and she's four years old," he exclaimed. "How can you do that to her?"

Oh yes, we've had our moments, this daughter of mine, but now that she's eighteen, our relationship has mellowed and deepened. She has come to understand and appreciate the choices that I've made, some of which have been very painful for her and her brother. And when she decided that she was going to college in New York, instead of playing it safe here in California, I said yes, without hesitation. Yes, flex your wings and fly, I told her, secretly thrilled by the possibility of living out my what-might-have-beens through her.

I became pregnant with Maia, my youngest child, when my marriage was in its last gasps and I was drowning in tears and anger. Yet, even as the uncertainty of my future bent me out of shape, some people saw my pregnancy as a good thing. "That child you are carrying will take you to new places," an elderly stranger told me.

The moment I finally had my little daughter in my arms, I felt a gigantic weight lift from my heart and a warm sense of well-being overpowered me. I don't know if it was her unusual alertness as a newborn or my relief that she wasn't deformed, but I was convinced that the clouds had lifted and my children and I were on our way to a new life. I wasn't wrong.

When Maia was nine months old (Carlo was 10 and Jaja, 8), we left the country to start life anew in a foreign land. It was a move that sprung not just from failure but more so from defiance. The odds were against us: a single mother and three small children didn't stand much of a chance, if you believe the statistics. True enough, it had not been easy but we have steered our way out of the fog. And in so doing, I was able to give back to my children what they have taught me: love, patience, and renewal in exchange for strength and endurance.

Fair enough, isn't it?

•*Businessworld Outpost*, June 1998•

The Big Night

HER ANNOUNCEMENT couldn't have come at a worse time.

There I was perched on the bathroom counter, trying to deny middle age by pulling out as much as I could of my white hairs that seemed to have grown overnight. And the wrinkles around my eyes! I was wallowing in self-pity when my then-fifteen-year-old daughter Jaja barged in.

"Mom, I'm going to the winter ball."

Long silence. I turned my head slowly, dramatically, the way Susan Roces would have done on finding out that her husband, Ronnie Poe, was having an affair. "Are you asking me if you can go to your winter ball?" I said.

My lame follow-up wasn't original. It was the same line my father used when I wanted to go to my junior-senior prom more than thirty years ago. At that time, in the Philippines, we had to meekly ask for our parents' permission to do something eventful. Mine often said no, and I would then run to my room in tears and call up my best friend. And that would be the end of it. Traditional Filipino parents like mine never tolerated arguments or questions about their decisions.

But this was America in the nineties, and Jaja, who has lived here since she was eight, was not restrained by the restrictions I suffered from. "No, Mom," she stressed. "I'm just letting you know that I'm going."

My mind assumed freeway speeds. What should I do now? Do I invoke Filipino culture and chastise her for being *lapastangan* (disrespectful)? Or should I remain calm and wait for a better time to give her a lecture on respecting one's elders and all that stuff? Maybe I should also throw in something about teenage boys and the danger of seduction?

Sensing that I was about to launch into a "when-I-was-young" story, Jaja quickly exited, but not before saying that she also needed to go shopping for a dress.

This must be a universal experience, the consternation a parent feels the first time a child declares that she's grown up. For me, because I had to deal with it alone—and in a culture quite different from what I grew up in—it felt like I had been hit by a tornado.

Will I let her wear a short, tight dress? Should I scrutinize her date's family background? Check his car? (An old car could be an excuse for being stranded somewhere, I knew.) Insist that another couple ride with them? Impose an 11 p.m. curfew?

I was in a dilemma because in my youth, my parents refused to allow me to wear a short dress, and my best friend and her date had to be with my date when he picked me up for the ball. At forty-five years old, I was still suffering from adolescent traumas, such as the extreme humiliation of having had strict parents.

The next two weeks before the big event were intense. Jaja and I shopped and argued—I wanted her to wear a sweet long-sleeved dress but she said, "yuck!" and bought a long, black gown with a see-through back. I wanted her date to visit before the actual night because I needed to be assured that he'd be well-behaved. She answered, "Mom, he's just a friend, and he's nice. Trust me on this."

What's a Filipino mother to do when her upbringing and experience clash with the prevailing mores of America in the nineties? In addition to my anxiety over my daughter's safety and the quality of my parenting, I was struggling with my own immaturity. As a mother, I was concerned about her date's driving. But as a post-adolescent forty five-year-old, I wondered if he was cute.

The big night came, and we, the doting family, positioned ourselves in strategic areas in the living room. My daughter and her girlfriend—at least I got this concession—who had been primping for hours, both looked so adorable in their grown-up clothes that by the time their dates showed up—late because they got lost—I was already feeling relaxed and almost triumphant. I had them pose for pictures, of course.

The boys were sweet and shy and didn't look like they were gang members or drunk drivers. They were supposed to be home by midnight, since the dance— held at the school gym—would end at 10:00 p.m. Enough time to eat out and maybe talk for a while, I figured. But Jaja called at 11:55 p.m. to say they were having fun with the rest of their Asian American circle at a restaurant close by and could she stay out until 1 a.m.?

She actually asked my permission, so I felt vindicated and immediately said, "Sure!" But, hanging up the phone, I remembered what I did when I went out on dates in college. Wait a minute, did I actually allow her to be away another hour?

But this is America in the nineties. Kids are so much wiser now... I hope.

•*Filipinas* Magazine, April 1997•

From Beethoven to the Beatles

WHEN I WAS expecting my first child and reading everything I could lay my hands on about children and parenthood, I came across an article that recommended playing Beethoven's Symphony No. 5 when babies are asleep. Apparently someone tested various music on infants and this particular work of Beethoven, more than any other, kept them calm and sleeping soundly.

And so when Carlo was born, I kept Symphony No. 5 playing on the stereo near him. It worked—he was a consistently sweet, even-tempered infant who made my first foray into parenthood easy and pleasurable.

Jaja was a different story altogether. Born with a mind of her own and a lot of attitude, no amount of Beethoven could calm her when she decided to exercise her lungs. I switched to various composers in desperation: Mozart, Brahms, Strauss, even Tchaikovsky, but nothing worked. Jaja would drown out the music with her crying, stopping only when she was too tired to go on.

After months of futile experimentation, my husband gave up on parenting theories and decided to just wing it. Carlo was already old enough to sleep on his own, without Beethoven, so classical music was out the window and in its stead, we had our daily dose of Bob Dylan. It was Bob Dylan for breakfast, lunch, dinner, and most of the hours in-between. We listened to him so much the maids memorized his words and could whip out "Like a Rolling Stone" just as well as they did Nora Aunor's "Pearly Shells."

Curiously, Jaja stayed calm whenever Dylan's music played. I don't know whether she was getting tired of asserting herself or the beat struck an elemental chord in her young mind. Perhaps she sensed that I was slowly going insane from trying to figure her out and listening to Dylan's laments at the same time. Whatever it was, the music strangely had a positive effect on her and we no longer had a colicky, screaming baby in our hands. [When Jaja started seriously listening to Bob Dylan in college, she felt that she already knew the words to his songs. It was weird, she said, because it almost felt like comfort food.]

Eight years later, when I had Maia, I declared our house Dylan-free and played instead the music I liked. My husband and our marriage had started to fade into the sunset so I had full control over the radio. This time it was DZRJ, which played the rock music of the '60s, and so I nursed Maia to the rhythm of "Light My Fire," lulled her to sleep on "Bridge Over Troubled Waters" and woke her up to Peter, Paul and Mary's "For Baby." It was great: the music soothed my troubled soul by transporting me back to a less complicated time and it gave Maia rhythm. Even before she could stand on her own, Maia was already rockin' on my lap as our music played.

Which brings me to what I want to confess to you today: I am a Beatles fanatic. Unabashed. Unapologetic. Though my musical taste has expanded through the years, and I don't listen to them as often as I did when I was young, whenever I need some soothing, nothing works as well for me as listening to the Fab Four.

From the time I first heard the synchopated one-two-three-four of "I Saw Her Standing There" in *Dancetime with Chito*, I was hooked. My world literally changed as I abandoned the mushiness of Paul Anka's "Puppy Love" and the Everly Brothers' "Devoted to You" and wholeheartedly embraced the "yeah yeah yeah" of "She Loves You" and the overpowering strangeness of John Lennon's "I heard the news today, oh boy..."

I was in high school when the Beatles became the biggest group on earth. Their songs accompanied our coming of age and chronicled our teenage joys and woes. Who could forget learning how to boogie with "I Don't Want to Spoil the Party" or playing the rhythm guitar with "Follow the Sun"? Whenever I'd get together with friends on weekends, we would inevitably end up singing such songs as "If I Fell," "P.S. I Love You," and "Do You Want to Know a Secret" while sipping Sarsi and ribbing each other about our crushes. I remember how our teacher-chaperones would turn eagle-eyed as the boys rushed to the girls of their choice when "Here, There, and Everywhere" played, well aware of the dangers of dancing too close and getting those raging adolescent hormones fired up.

The years have not erased the elemental thrill I feel whenever I hear the initial strum of John Lennon's guitar in "A Hard Day's Night." I watched that movie with my best friend one summer afternoon. We were just supposed to spend the day at her house but instead, sneaked out to Holiday Theater in Santa Mesa—just us two, without an adult—and screamed ourselves hoarse along with the rest of the audience. My parents never found out about this escapade and to this day I savor the forbidden excitement of that first rebellion, no matter how lame, compared to the things I would eventually be doing.

These days, when there's a lull in our online chats, my old friends and I sometimes break into virtual singing. One of us would start by typing the first line of a song and the rest would pick up where the others left off. It's fun, it's silly; our children would probably be embarrassed if they find out. But for us aging boomer babes, it transports us back to the time when we would sing the Beatles' "In My Life" ("There are places I remember/all my life/ though some have changed") not realizing that the song would still speak for us, about us, thirty-five years later: "All these places have their moments/ through lovers and friends I still can recall/ some are dead and some are living/ in my life, I've loved them all."

•*Filipinas* Magazine, May 2001•

Letting Go

MY TWELVE-YEAR-OLD daughter Maia, who grew up humming and swaying to the quintessential song of my childhood, "Puff the Magic Dragon," is now actually singing it and accompanying herself on the guitar. The first time she understood the lyrics, she was surprised that it is such a sad song, speaking as it does of the loss of a best friend.

Nothing prepared her, however, for what her guitar teacher told her as they were playing the song together—it is actually about a kite! This revelation made Maia cry because she had always believed the song to be about an imaginary magical friend, not something as mundane as a kite.

I tried to temper her disappointment by saying that Puff could be whatever she wanted it to be but the blow had been dealt, another piece of her innocence lost forever.

Welcome to the grown-up world, darling, where losses are as inevitable as moonrise and sunsets, and we must constantly struggle to let go as gracefully as we can manage. It is never easy.

We all know the litany: The end of childhood, relationships terminated, opportunities lost, loves that turned to hate, death. The little losses are easily brushed away, but the big ones occupy a space in our being, each becoming another layer of defense against the heartaches that tend to come, often at inopportune times.

Those of us in the "sandwich" generation—with kids to raise and aging parents to care for—have come to accept the inevitability of loss. We steel our hearts in anticipation and do all we can to be ready, even as we know that we can never be truly prepared.

A friend dropped off her youngest son at his college of choice thousands of miles away, leaving her and her husband with an empty nest in a strange country, devoid of the sounds and smells of an adolescent-in-residence.

Those of us who have escorted a child to college know the feeling well. We go about arming our children with everything we think they will need and want—comforter, food, storage bins, underwear—hoping that these will not only assuage their homesickness but also lessen our sense of loss.

We fight the need to let go, fiercely at first. We call, we mail care packages, we send money. But no amount of denial can change what we know deep in our hearts—that our children as we know them are gone forever. When they come back—to visit—they will be adults with lives and dreams of their own, and all we can do is pray that we have given them enough wind to power their wings.

When my childhood buddy lost her last remaining parent, an all too familiar loss for our generation, she knew it was coming and she had braced herself for it. But when the dreaded call-in-the-middle-of-the-night came, she was still devastated. Both my parents passed away in the first two years after my move to the US and I know the shock and the helplessness of knowing that death is thousands of miles away. I had to endure an agonizingly long plane ride before I could even begin to mourn.

Losses.

I was feeling brave and nostalgic one cold night so I dug out my journal of my last year in college from a pile of mementos I have carried with me through all the moves I have made. I have kept journals of various phases of my life, and have reread most of them except that one. It was the one that told the story of the most painful loss I had endured, when I was young and naive, and not yet aware of such grown-up concepts as betrayal and heartbreak.

I leafed through the entries that were obviously written amidst an intense emotional roller coaster ride and I was alternately amused and saddened that the girl who had gone through that upheaval and had written with such passion had become a stranger. Silly of me to think that dredging up that part of my past thirty years later could bring back the same searing pain. I had feared that pain, and tried never again to think back to that time. Now I discovered that that fear was all for naught, that the layers of defenses I have built up through the years have succeeded in erasing whatever lingering feelings I thought I still harbored.

Today as I watch Maia sleeping peacefully beside me, blissfully unaware of what still lies ahead, I make my own wish. May you, my dear child, always have a magic dragon to keep you centered as you trudge through your own losses, and your own kite to show you that to let go is to set yourself free.

•*Filipinas* Magazine, October 2000•

Paternal Instincts

I'M NOT A "Hallmark holiday" kind of person. I have never voluntarily or willfully celebrated Valentine's Day in my life, not even in my younger, more romantically inclined, years. And I don't like Mother's Day because I find it too manufactured and commercialized, despite its being a long-standing tradition. (Besides, if my children only honor me once a year on a date determined by the greeting card industry, I will be rightfully upset.)

I ease up a bit though when it comes to Father's Day, even if I mistakenly thought that it was another one of those newly created, money-baiting marketing schemes. (Did you know that the first public Father's Day celebration was in 1909 and President Lyndon Johnson officially designated the third Sunday of June as such in 1966?) I think it's cute to have a once-a-year tribute to fathers especially in this day and age when it's awfully difficult to be a dad—especially if you're a mom.

Like all single parents, the demarcation line between being a father and being a mother has long ago disappeared. I have gotten so used to this duality that, try as I may, I can no longer imagine a different life, where parenting decisions are shared, areas of responsibilities are divided, and the joy of parenting is not tempered by exhaustion from having to be two persons at the same time. Just being able to get through a day without a major mishap was already reason to celebrate.

My older children's teenage years were a character builder, for them and for me. We loved and fought with equal ferocity, each of us unsure of how we should play our roles yet conscious of the need to assume multiple ones to keep the family ship on an even keel. I still feel guilty when I remember how my son, who was only ten when his father and I separated, had to take on adult tasks, like mowing the lawn and taking care of his younger sisters, at a time when he should have been a carefree kid. Did I rob him and his sister of their childhoods because of my decision to break free?

The need to be a father assumed a bigger dimension in their teenage years when my older daughter started dating and my son was going through the often-painful search for identity. I was entering highly emotional and basically unfamiliar territory, something that drew out in me the lingering traumas of my own youth.

Having had a very conservative and emotionally distant father, I was a natural rebel against dating traditions and anything that smacked of authoritarianism. While a Filipino father would be strict and scary to the boys who hovered around his daughter and who wanted to take her out, I was torn between sternness and permissiveness, knowing full well how, as a teenage girl, I felt embarrassed when my father insisted that I not get into a car alone with a boy. I remember how I longed to be trusted by my parents and I wanted to give my then sixteen-year-old daughter my full trust.

Yet there was a part of me that reflected my parents' anxiety: what if the boy was not trustworthy? Should I have done what one Filipino father in central California did before his daughter's first date—took the boy out to dinner and read him the Riot Act?

Raising a son was an entirely different ballgame: I just didn't know how! I pored over parenting books and asked my friends for whatever tips they could give. But ultimately, I realized that there were no instructional manuals, nothing to make me understand completely the growing pains that my son was going through. I went by my instincts and braced myself for the inevitable clashes, willing myself the strength to ignore the Mohawk haircuts, the ridiculous outfits, the sullen teenage expressions, the coming-home-at-dawn and sleeping-all-morning. I kept reminding myself to allow him these little rebellions so long as he did not end up in prison or rehab.

Then my son and daughter reached driving age. It was the one rite of passage that I considered a father's domain but I had no choice but to preside over it—be the one who sat beside them barking instructions as they tentatively negotiated their way through the streets of our neighborhood, as well as the treacherous alleys of pre-adulthood. They were on their way to freedom while I was a nervous wreck, scared of the dangers they would face, and distressed at the prospect of loosening the parental heartstrings.

Some weeks ago my three kids and I were together for a few days— a rare occasion now since my older daughter, who is twenty-four, has been living on the other coast for years. My son is now twenty-six, my youngest daughter sixteen. We are a family welded more tightly by the many burnings we had to go through.

It warmed my heart to see them, who were once my crosses, independently and determinedly forging their way toward their own chosen lives. And I give thanks for everything that we have been given. Everything, including the chance for me to be their mother and father at the same time.

•*Filipinas* Magazine, June 2004•

Empty Nesting

FOUR DAYS AFTER Jaja moved into her New York college dorm, on the day Maia and I were flying home to California after taking her there, I realized that my older daughter had already learned what it meant to be a starving student.

"Can you have the rest of that meatloaf wrapped for my dinner?" she asked as we were finishing lunch. I felt my stomach lurch and my eyes water: She hates meatloaf, never ate it, even when it was garnished with good spices. I panicked at the thought of her going hungry. Being a Filipino mother, my first instinct was to rush to the store and buy a cartful of groceries.

But Jaja, being Jaja, nixed the food shopping and insisted on buying a comforter instead. "Don't worry about me," she asserted, but in the same breath, added that it would be turning cold soon and she would really need the comforter.

On the plane a few hours later, I would reach for Maia's hand whenever I felt the lump in my throat threaten to spill over as tears. "Are you okay, Mama?" my sensitive ten-year-old asked several times. Though I would say yes, she wasn't convinced. My face must have registered the conflict in my heart: On the one hand I was so proud that my older daughter had the strength to strike out on her own; on the other, I was scared that her 18 years of knowledge and attitude (along with whatever advice she allowed herself to take from me) would not be enough to carry her through the pain and the confusion that adulthood imposes on everyone. Especially when she's so far away.

In one memorable argument we had a few years back, I demanded that Jaja listen to me so she would not make the same mistakes I made.

"Mom, you'll have to allow me to make my own mistakes," she retorted.

"Oh, but you will, you will, whether you like it or not," I insisted. "What I'm saying is that you should save yourself the trouble of repeating my mistakes."

For a while it seemed like I was talking to the wall, but months later, she showed me an essay she wrote for class about how she had come to understand and appreciate the way I have chosen to live my life. Yeeeesss, she got it, I exulted.

These thoughts come back as I struggle to keep from constantly checking up on Jaja, all alone (well, in a manner of speaking) in Manhattan. I maintain e-mail correspondence with my friends in the area, reminding them that she's there and to please, please call her up occasionally to make sure she isn't starving.

Meanwhile, at the home front, I am developing a newfound patience with my two other children. I try, for example, to get off Carlo's case, knowing that in a year's time, he too will be off on his own. But even now, with only one member of the family away, I sometimes feel like I am in a giant abyss—the house is too big, too quiet for comfort. When Carlo leaves, will I be able to appreciate the increased space and the greater solitude? For someone who has never spent a night alone in a house (in the Philippines, there was at least a maid to keep me company), the prospect is daunting.

And yet, when I'm in a bad mood or my children are occupying more of my space than I am willing to concede, I wish to fast-forward to the time when they're living independently. "Hurry and grow up," I would tell them, tactlessly. "I want my own life back." But is there really a taking one's life back when one is a parent?

I never had a second thought about agreeing to Jaja's moving away. This is, in fact, what I had prepared them for, what my child-rearing strategy has been about. Ever since they took their first steps and I watched them struggle to keep their balance and resisted from stopping them from falling. "Every experience is a lesson," I have always said.

With this mantra defining my motherhood, I made sure their experiences were varied and real. I never shielded them from the imperfections of people and the ugliness in the world, so they could learn tolerance and appreciate beauty.

Before she moved to her dorm, I told Jaja that there are only three things I ask of her: That she not get pregnant before she's ready, that she doesn't pick up an incurable disease, and that she lives by the Golden Rule every minute of her life. "Beyond these rules, you are free to live your life the way you want," I stressed, secretly keeping my fingers crossed.

Meanwhile, in my better moments, I celebrate. One less kid to worry about, two more to go, I would joke. More often now, when uncertainty and anxiety creep in, I savor the memory of what my friend, the late poet Alfrredo Navarro Salanga, once told me. "You're a mother who doesn't smother," he said.

I cherish that compliment. I just hope that my children will, one day, see me the same way.

Filipinas Magazine, November 1998•

On the Road

THIRTEEN YEARS AGO, when I was deciding on moving to the Bay Area from Manila with my three children, one of the exciting possibilities that I looked forward to was taking roadtrips with them. Just the four of us. I would just get them in the car on a weekend, throw some clothes and sleeping bags in the trunk, pack some snacks then off we'd go. The destination was not important; it was the freedom to take flight spontaneously, the way Cher did in the movie *Mermaids*, that made the idea so attractive.

But alas, real life is not quite that cinematic. In our early years, our few roadtrips always involved other relatives. Not only was it cheaper, it was safer. When Carlo and Jaja became teenagers, no amount of cajoling (Disneyland? San Diego Zoo? Snow?) could entice them to be cooped up in a car for long stretches and so my dream of a Jack Kerouac-like odyssey-with-a-twist slowly faded.

Until two months ago when Carlo decided to move to a city eight hours away. He wanted our help in looking for a place there, so a roadtrip with just the four of us was finally the unavoidable option. The timing couldn't have been more perfect: Jaja had just come back from a five-month backpacking journey through three continents and Maia was on summer vacation. We all needed some time with each other, so I grabbed the chance to reclaim my dream of cruising the great highways together, with the big blue sky above us, while the CD player blared our music. The thrill of escape has never quite left me.

This roadtrip was also a good time to get to know each other better. Carlo and Jaja are now grown-ups and in the process of carving their own niches, independent of me. I was missing the openness I thought we had when they were children, and I was hoping to recapture that. I got more than I bargained for.

This particular conversation started with stories about their growing up in Quezon City. "We had such a happy childhood, Mom," Jaja declared. "That was why the pain of our uprooting was almost unbearable." It was the first time my kids spoke of the agony of our first years here and I realized they had intentionally hid the truth from me because they knew I was also going through my own suffering. We are past that dark period now, so we were able to talk about it openly. It still wasn't easy but the relief that we collectively felt was immensely gratifying.

A few days after we came home, Jaja handed me this letter, which I am sharing with you (with her permission). I hope that it will help Filipino immigrant parents understand where their resentful and possibly misbehaving children are coming from as they try to adjust to the realities of life in America.

> *I hated that we came here. We can all giggle now at Kuya's little quip about how we were tricked into moving to America, but it's true. You never could have gotten me to move willingly.*
>
> *Three days into the new life, I already knew that it was unacceptable. Everything was wrong. The food was tasteless and disgusting, the people were all empty smiles and loud voices, the weather unbearable. And I actually had to do the laundry and dishes? I could only handle this for a year, I thought, but for you, Mama, I'd stay for two. But that's it.*
>
> *And for two years my only reality was dreaming about the day when I would go back to the Philippines. My only comfort from American life was that one day, it would all end. One day, I would no longer have to stand alone in the playground—the only kid who dreaded the recess bell. One day, I wouldn't have teachers speaking to*

me slowly, in loud voices. I'd have friends again. One day, I would no longer be tempted to break the dishes as I washed them.

But that day two years later never came. Or rather, it did come but instead of bringing with it plane tickets and polvoron, it was just another Thanksgiving and more disappointment than could possibly, humanely, be meant for an 11-year-old girl. It was a nightmare— absurd, disorienting, and just too bad to be true. But the worst part was being told that it didn't matter whether I was convinced that this was true or not. Either way I wasn't getting out of it.

After that, much to your relief, I stopped throwing tantrums. In fact, I stopped everything. My classmates used to ignore me because they thought I didn't speak English; now, they ignored me because I didn't speak. I began by believing that everything in America was wrong— wrong food, wrong people, wrong houses, wrong weather. Now I just believed I was wrong—wrong clothes, wrong accent, wrong childhood, wrong life. My compromise had turned into blind, supplicating resignation. For years, I was described as shy. I wasn't shy. I was defeated.

It took years, Jaja said, before she was able to let go of her bitterness. When she finally did (and she doesn't remember how it happened), it felt like a new world had opened up.

But I'm healed now. I woke up one day and—surprise—I haven't thought about my heartbreak in months.

Describe me as you will but there is no resemblance anymore between the present me and that listless and lonely teenager.

I guess Jaja finally figured out that sometimes what you get is better than what you wanted in the first place.

•*Filipinas* Magazine, October 2001•

Call of the Wild

JUST WHEN my two older children have moved out to lives of their own, my youngest child becomes a teenager. We all know how that is, right? Our normally sweet and obedient child turns sullen and rebellious one moment, then switches back to being a little kid the next. The pattern can go on until they find their *barkada* (peer group) and start giving way to their raging hormones. Then we start wondering how the little angel has become a stranger and, depending on our worry meter, we either lose sleep or wait patiently in the background, ready to provide succor when they slip and fall.

Maia is much younger than her older siblings and I raised her without her biological father, so I feel (rightly or wrongly) that however she turns out is a reflection of my parenting skills. Her success is my success, her failure my failure, that sort of thing. I know that puts an unfair burden on Maia and I'm trying my best to spare her from my parental eccentricity. Yet, because she has been such a sweetheart, I can't help but strut secretly in self-congratulation.

So far so good, I tell myself. But lately, I've been thinking, "Here we go again" as she begins her own adolescent journey. I was not as present as I wanted to be during my older kids' teenage years because it happened when my main focus was to keep the family operation (i.e., feeding, clothing, educating) going and I hardly had enough energy left to try and fathom the turbulence in their hearts. And I regret it to this day because I would have learned much from them, and Carlo and Jaja would probably have picked up a lesson or two from their mother's choices.

Now that it's Maia's turn, I feel like I'm dealing with an adolescent for the first time and I'm quite anxious. True, I have help now—from her siblings, my in-laws, and an entire community of high school classmates that I am constantly in touch with. But when Maia started getting calls from boys, and when she asks if she can meet up with friends at the mall, I am momentarily stumped. Is she old enough? Will she be safe? Will I be a bad parent if I'm too permissive?

Years ago, when Jaja declared that she was going to her first ball at fifteen, I vacillated between strictness and excitement, not only because it was new territory and I remembered well my frustration when my father refused to allow me to attend parties. It was also because I was still scrambling to undo my adolescent traumas while trying to figure out how to raise teenagers in this new age and new world where the traditions that we were reared by have become incongruous, if not passé.

The good thing about going through teenage parenting at that time was that my friends were going through the same thing so we shared our dilemmas and worked them out together. One particularly wrenching one was "the first boyfriend." We stumbled our way on that one because it just felt so strange to be dealing with the issue as parents when the memory of our first relationships—and everything that they involved—were still so fresh in our minds. We laughed so hard when a friend in Manila took to canceling his appointments and staying home when his daughter's boyfriend came to visit, because he was afraid the guy would do the same things he did when he was visiting his girlfriend. Our mirth, of course, was tinged with embarrassment because we were, in our own style, doing the same watchful thing.

A few years back, when on a *balikbayan* visit, Carlo and Jaja unearthed my teenage diaries from a box of mementos that I wanted them to bring back to the States. Against their better judgment (their words), they read some of my entries, which surprisingly were very detailed descriptions of my thoughts and feelings at that time.

"Eeeweeoooo, Mama, it's gross how you were so boy-crazy," they exclaimed on the phone. "Stop reading them," I yelled, but it was too late. They were already on to their mother's past.

On hindsight, however, it was good because when they came back they were more open to me about their own thoughts and feelings, marking a major shift in their attitude towards me from distance to closeness. As Jaja said, while they would have preferred to not know about my many crushes, she was happy that I was now de-mystified. "I'm glad to know you were just as confused as I am," she sighed.

I use the same tested approach with Maia now. Every chance I get I talk to her about what her *ate* and *kuya* had to go through with me when they were her age, and what I had to go through with my own parents. The contrast between the two parenting styles always catches her interest and she can be effusive with her gratitude that I am not unreasonably strict and that I prefer to trust rather than punish her. So far so good.

I dread the day though, as I dreaded it in the past, when she falls in love and I will have to tread the delicate balance between protecting her from being hurt and encouraging the exuberance of young love. But I also await that day with excitement because, like a true Baby Boomer parent who still daydreams about romantic encounters, I want to share with her my own cache of memories about the earth-shaking, life-defining thrill of First Love.

•*Filipinas* Magazine, February 2002•

Grandparental Moments

I WAS uncharacteristically purposive about my destination as I strode briskly across the mall, hardly conscious of the hordes around me. And then it happened: I heard a baby cry. I heard it over the cacophony of sounds in such a public place, over the chatter, the boisterous laughter, the loud music, the voices hawking stuff and an organ playing.

Normally, the sound of one baby crying does not stand a chance of being heard in this kind of situation except by the parents, but I heard it loudly, clearly and I had to stop. The baby could not have been more than six months old and it was obviously hungry. I watched as the mother gently lifted him from the stroller and gave him the bottle. It was definitely a Kodak moment.

I stood there and watched as the infant sucked furiously and then turned his face away, content now and gurgling happily. As his mother turned him upright to burp him, and he started smiling at those around him I was tempted to walk over to ask if I could carry him, just for a moment, to appease the intense longing I felt just then for a baby to embrace.

What's going on here? Is there a biological clock that ticks for grandparents?

Some years back, my friend Lory and I were people-watching at a park and noting the many young men and women pushing strollers or running after their toddlers, we asked each other, " Do we miss those days?" And spontaneously, emphatically we said, "Of course not." We had just been updating one another about our children and we had breathed sighs of relief and regret in equal measure that they are finally about fully grown and we are almost free from the intense, closed-in parenting that their younger years required.

It can be heady, this newly acquired semi-freedom. When I booked myself on a trip without having to take my youngest child along, I could not believe the lightness I felt. I could stay out late, I could choose not to eat. I could go anywhere I wanted without hearing a complaint. Heck, I could even watch an adult show! It was almost like growing up and moving out of your parents' house; the possibilities were endless.

The excitement, however, was short-lived. As soon as I arrived at my destination, I was on the phone calling home, checking if my daughter did her homework, if she ate a good dinner, if she brushed her teeth. And if she missed me. Since I was also far away from my two adult children, I likewise felt the need to check on them, fearing that the bond that kept them tethered to me would be severed if I didn't call. Habits die hard, especially for parents.

Much to my children's relief, I'm now more able to cut loose and actually enjoy myself without them. Admittedly, there are times when I overdo this, when they actually complain that they hardly see me anymore. Given the choice between my staying home constantly and my having a life separate from them, however, they would unhesitatingly choose the latter. "It's nice to see you not too grouchy," my irreverent daughter once commented.

And then grandparenting happened. Not to me but to many of my friends. Suddenly I started getting e-mails waxing poetic about the joys of having grandchildren. It's different, it's indescribable, I was told. "I should have had [my grandchild] first," Ray, writing from Manila, quipped.

The Christmas pictures that I got last year showed a lot of expanded families, with a toddler or two prominently seated on the laps of beaming *lolos* and *lolas*. These were the people I used to hang out with, we were teenagers together and did a lot of crazy stuff together. And they are now grandparents? I was alternately appalled and amused. How could they look so pleased and contented when the mere existence of their *apos* was a reminder of their age? But the stories of grandchildren kept coming and pretty soon, I started to feel left out, the way I felt left out more than twenty years ago when all my closest friends were getting married and having children, and I was still single.

The curious thing is that these new grandparents are uniformly and endearingly shameless about their offsprings' offspring. My friends in Canada, for example, display their granddaughter's picture everywhere including their press cards. Another had his grandson on stage with him when he accepted an award. Most everyone else I know will flash their grandchildren's photo every chance they get and will have to be stopped before they cease talking about them. "With our own children, we were too tense and scared to enjoy the moment," someone explained. Now they're making up for lost time.

Since I'm, hopefully, years away from having grandchildren of my own, I still can't relate too much to such unabashed enthusiasm. But this much I admit: there are days when I have a longing so deep to hold and care for a baby again, it's almost too hard to bear.

But it is good to know that I can return the child when my longing passes. And no more sleepless nights for me.

None of the responsibility, all of the joy. This is probably why grandparenting is so attractive. On this Mother's Day, here's a toast to all you *lolos* and *lolas* out there.

And to my children: don't even think about it ... yet.

•Filipinas Magazine, May 2002•

Taboo or Not Taboo

LET'S TALK about sex.

How many parents out there have not/would not/cannot utter these words to their children? I'm guessing most. In the arena of openness, which, if parenting books are to be believed, is one of the standards by which good parenting is measured, Filipino parents would fail miserably. It doesn't take much to understand why sexual queasiness is so ingrained in the Filipino. There's the Catholic Church, for one. We grew up under its puritan shadow, constantly told that sex and sin are synonymous, except in the only acceptable instance when a married couple is seeking to procreate. And even then, it would still be sinful to have sex if it involved preventing a pregnancy using "unnatural methods." Merely thinking about sex is already a no-no. In other words, the only sex that can be enjoyed without having to confess it to a priest (who is only supposed to know about the topic in theoretical terms) is the one that is sanctioned by a marriage license and only at a certain time of the month. Beyond that period, sex with contraceptives is a sin.

Our own parents were not much help. They belonged to a generation where the only S word allowed was "shssh" or the more emphatic "shut up." I don't think they discussed sex among themselves, even in hushed tones. Talking about it with their children was almost blasphemous and simply wasn't done. Thus we grew up naïve, repressed, and guilty but the taboo made the topic so wickedly delicious that we sought to find out more about it, surreptitiously of course, from sources that distorted and titillated. The social mores when I was growing up were just as inhospitable to a frank and honest approach to sex. Sure we had our biology lessons that described how a sperm and an egg meet to form a fetus, but it was not quite clear (at least not to me) how sperms united with eggs in the first place, and the emotional, social and physical dimensions of that phenomenon. What messages we got instead were prohibitions. We were not to go closer than a foot when dancing with guys (a high school teacher would even bring a ruler to dances and pry apart couples who dared defy her measurements), nice girls should not allow themselves to be touched no matter how innocently, and we were not to make references to anything sexual lest we be tagged as rude or loose.

I find it so refreshing to see young people today greeting each other with casual hugs and being so unself-conscious about saying "I love you" to their close friends, which was unthinkable during our time.

We were so constricted by tradition that an accidental brushing of hands with the opposite sex made our hearts beat fast, a mere glance from our crushes sent us into ecstasies, and a few words exchanged became subjects of our daydreams for days. We laugh about it now, my high school classmates and I, who have finally found our comfort level with each other and are now more open about discussing sex (or in most instances, the lack of it). The guys tell us about how the combination of raging hormones, shyness, peer pressure, lack of information and just sheer adventurousness led them to the prostitution dens of Pasay to establish their manhood as a group.

And us girls double up with laughter as they recall how, without our being aware of it, their imaginations ran wild when they saw us in our short skirts and our ugly bloomers (physical education uniforms). Because we were so painfully shy with each other then, we now marvel at the ease with which we kissed and hugged, unshackled finally from the sexual tensions that confused us as kids.

Are our children better off now that we have loosened up somewhat from the rigidity of our upbringing? I have a feeling most Filipino parents are still shy about discussing sex directly, perhaps because most are still not comfortable or very aware of the full measure of their own sexualities. We may openly joke with our friends about it but when posed questions by our kids, we tend to clam up or speak in generalities so that we don't have to confront our own ambivalence, or ignorance. I know because when my two older children were going through their adolescence, I left it to their schools and the media to make them aware of sex and its consequences.

The only time I actually talked about it was when I told my daughter, who was going away to college, that all I was asking of her was to avoid getting an incurable illness (meaning AIDS or STD) and not to get pregnant. I remember saying it breezily, like I was reminding her to take her vitamins, because I was avoiding a discussion about it.

Apparently, Filipino parents, as a demographic, are not doing enough to instill in their children a healthy consciousness of responsible sex, judging from statistics indicating that teen pregnancy and AIDS are highest among Filipino American youths, compared to other Asian groups.

So let's all get over it and talk to our children about what we should know by now: That making good love is about the most soul-satisfying, sublime act that human beings are capable of doing with a partner they care deeply about.

Let's spare them the burden of guilt trips and misinformation and tell them that for as long as they do it responsibly and caringly, sex is something they should celebrate with full hearts and open minds.

And then maybe we can believe it ourselves.

•*Filipinas* Magazine, August 2004•

friends & lovers

Karma Chameleon

IT IS MY KIND of day and my kind of leisure, sitting in a sidewalk café with a friend from way back, sipping good coffee while taking in the sounds of this beautiful city. I glance at N, sitting right across me, looking alternately captivated and miserable. Has it already been ten minutes since we sat down?

My mind, for a while, is not in San Francisco. It is back home when we were both much younger, in Quezon City, Ayala Avenue, Roxas Boulevard at midnight, a rally or two at the U.S. Embassy. Visions of our shared past tumbling back at a furious pace, like a slide show gone awry. This is the guy who could once define my day, whose name littered the pages of my teenage diary.

Now, when we both have had our separate share of heartbreaks and triumphs, unwanted pounds and backaches, the sexual tensions of our youth have cooled to a deep and comfortable friendship. In fact, he is here to continue a conversation we started nine years ago, a few days before I left for America.

Then, he was at the top of his career and his life was one big party. He was earning so much money and was spending it with abandon. The house that he built for his family (wife, two small children) was so ostentatious, it jarred my pedestrian tastes. I found it particularly obscene that the garage, where he sheltered his collection of cars and motorcycles, was larger than my house.

He was leaving the country for a two-year assignment and was swelling with the thrill of anticipated adventure and illicit romance. Just like many at his power level, he had a young, pretty girlfriend whom he treated like a trophy. Because he thought he was invincible and the world was his to conquer, he had no qualms about taking her with him, leaving his family in Manila to await his quarterly visits.

It was the wrong time to break his plans to me. I was then going through marital hell and had transformed into this witch of a woman who raged against the entire universe and ranted against the arrogance and irresponsibility of Filipino macho men, who thought it their God-given right to discard their wives, their children, their morals "just like that," to shack up with young, brainless gold diggers who would eventually leave them for younger, more virile men! "Who do you think you are," I needled him. "Who gave you the right to mess up other people's lives?"

Through the entire lunch, I was vile and self-righteous, unreasonable—and unstoppable. I laced the sumptuous dishes he ordered with the venom of my bitterness; the mango shake curdled with my anger. Looking back, I'm still amazed that our kinship survived that encounter.

He proved to be a truer friend than I thought.

Knowing that I was hurting and struggling to start a new life in America, he would call and write reassuring letters, never ever mentioning our last encounter. Eventually, when my negativity dissipated and I could truly say I had put my former life behind me, I wrote back affectionate letters wishing him love and fulfillment.

When he called to say he would be flying into San Francisco for a few days and that we had to talk, I knew immediately that the wheel had turned, as I (somewhat maliciously) predicted it would.

He tells me that the sweet young thing he brought with him, like designer luggage, to his foreign post has long ago flown and he's had other short-lived dalliances since. His career has reached its apex and his company now treats him like a senior official, revered but no longer given challenges. "And I'm not even fifty yet!" he says, ruefully.

Finally, the clincher, worthy of a Christopher de Leon/Vilma Santos starrer: His wife has found out about his faithlessness and is threatening to leave him. He is hurt and confused; like many Filipino males in the

Philippines, he does not know how to deal with emotional turmoil. For the first time in his life, this corporate hotshot is not in control.

"I gave her everything she ever wanted. Why is she doing this to me?" he asks miserably.

Excuse me! I start to say something but I bite into my croissant instead.

It is the nature of our relationship that we alternate as listener to each other's laments. I also sense that he wants me to get mad so he can sit there and take it, and perhaps feel that he is atoning for something. Ah, but his story is much too common back home where infidelity and self-indulgence are accepted as part of the bounty of success.

Listening to him now in this cozy café ten thousand miles from where we started, I feel alternately sad and relieved that this buddy of mine, this bundle of contradictions sitting right across me, now realizes that he is just as flawed and as accountable as everyone else.

•*Filipinas* Magazine, October 1997•

Take Back the Light

I WOULD LIKE to share with you this letter I sent to a close friend, whose situation is familiar to many women.

Dearest Claire,

So your husband beat you up again, for the seventh time, you say? That is seven times too many! Strange that you're actually keeping a tally. Is it because you are giving him a limit before you start doing something about your marriage? Or are you still trying to convince yourself that being your husband's punching bag seven times in eighteen years of marriage is not too bad? What about the constant put-downs, the verbal abuse, his infidelities, don't they count too?

Claire, how much longer are you going to take this? Look intently at yourself in the mirror; don't you see a frightened, haggard woman, old beyond her years staring back at you? What happened to the feisty lady who could stare down military goons and dirty old men? It pains me so much to see you now, you who were always the wisest and most mature in our *barkada*.

I know we should be asking ourselves what happened to our youthful dreams and illusions, but I won't get into that because right now I am seething with anger. At what's-his-face for killing your spirit. And at you for taking it and conjuring such ridiculous excuses to justify your staying with him. Okay, I know you're feeling miserable right now but I want to remind you of what you used to say when he decorated your body with bruises. Ready?

"I deserved it." Of all the idiotic statements that you ever uttered, this is the most pathetic. Nobody deserves to be beaten up, Claire, even if you did something wrong (which you didn't). If he is angry about something, you and he should talk. Like adults. If that's too hard, then get a third party to mediate. But he has no right to take out his aggressions on you.

"He hasn't done this for a long time." What? Does this mean that if he limits himself to one beating every three years, it will be okay? When will it not be okay, when he does it twice a year?

"He's under too much stress." Okay. Do you beat him or your children up when you are stressed out? Does he think a marriage license entitles him to use you as his punching bag? Stress is a given and if everyone deals with it by beating up their spouses, then we would all be dead. Intelligent, mature people listen to music, talk it out, do meditation, watch a movie. Stupid lowlives take it out on others.

Claire, years ago, you told us that his verbal and physical cruelties had wiped away any joy left in your happy moments. And he had always broken his promise of not hurting you again. At that time, we still were not sure which prospect was scarier, suffering another beating or growing old alone. But that was then, when we didn't know any better and the unwritten rule for Filipino women was that we should stick with our marriages, no matter what. (Remember how somebody "advised" me to just hang on, wait it out, let my philandering husband "sow his wild oats" because he will, in the end, come back to me, his real wife? Wasn't that the height of absurdity?)

I know that the major reason you are choosing to suffer through what you yourself say is "a dead marriage" is that you believe it is best for the kids. Parenting books, priests and our elders have brainwashed us about this. Claire, they lie. Children are worse off when they see their parents constantly quarrelling, when there is no love in the marriage.

Neither is it true that children of broken homes always become messed up. Such children can and do thrive, even—or maybe especially—in a single-parent household so long as the main parent is strong and steadfast. And you are that kind of parent, Clarita, if you take away the fear that petrifies you now. Besides, by allowing yourself to be victimized, what kind of example are you giving your daughter?

As for the fear of growing old alone, remember what you told me ten years ago, when I was confronted by my then-husband's betrayal? "Don't worry," you said, "we will live out our lives like the Golden Girls." You can't imagine how that prospect sustained me through my difficult years, Claire, and I'm talking to you now as a survivor. It is lonelier to be in a relationship that doesn't work than to be actually alone. Trust me on this.

You know what really scares me? It's watching the light slowly die in your eyes. I want to see the Claire that I grew up with, not the depressed, defeated (and bruised) woman that you have allowed yourself to be. Let go, dearest friend. Come back to life!

Much love,
G.

•*Filipinas* Magazine, March 1998•
Runner-up, Opinion/Commentary Writing,
New California Media, San Francisco, 1999

Some Never Learn

I REMEMBER quite vividly what I was doing when Ninoy Aquino was assassinated in 1983.

It was a warm, sunny Sunday afternoon in August, I was alone at home—family in Baguio, maids in Rizal Park—and I had all the time in the world to indulge in nostalgia and, in the process, massage my ego. The radio was on full blast with the Beatles as I dug through my collection of teenage memorabilia that I had kept hidden from prying eyes in a wooden trunk.

The trove included lots of photos—some already yellowed—taken during college fairs and other campus events, ticket stubs of memorable movies and concerts, paper bags from U.S. department stores, and notes from friends. And then there was the box of love letters that I had received through the years, which I had kept separate from the rest of the junk for reasons of conceit and expediency. Whenever I felt low or angry with my then-husband, I would surreptitiously take that box out and re-read the letters, remembering the times when I was pursued by guys, most of whom I couldn't even recall.

On that particular afternoon, as I unfolded one written on blue stationery, I heard the music interrupted by a flash announcement: Ninoy's plane had landed but no one had seen him disembark, there were reports of gunshots heard. Then an obviously distraught Doy Laurel came on, they were looking for Ninoy but no one seemed to know where he was. And those gunshots . . .

I sat there petrified, unbelieving. Soon I started sobbing. I didn't know what upset me more: Marcos's cruelty, Ninoy's possible martyrdom, or the murder of the English language by this person whose letter I was still holding.

"Dearest Gemma," it started. "I liked to talk to you at the library yesterday, but I am shy. Now I regretting (*sic*) because it is already summer vacation and I will not see you again until June. I will missed you (*sic*). I will always think of your lovly (*sic*) face in this summer. Love forever." The name was not even familiar. He either remained too shy to get to know me or his promise of forever only lasted until the next "lovly" face came his way.

Having grown up in the late '60s, my girlfriends and I were caught in the cusp of overly authoritarian parents—who did not allow us to talk to boys too long on the phone or, in my case, to ride in a car alone with a boy—and the increasingly perceptible wave of permissiveness and rebellion that would reach their crescendo during the First Quarter Storm in Manila in the early '70s.

Thus, though we were boy-crazy and did not think twice about defying our parents by going out on a lunch date alone with a boy in his car, we also played it coy when it came to those we really liked. Or those who were persistent enough to really woo us.

In college at UP, two pretty girl cousins my age lived with my parents and me in a cottage on campus. Since we were forbidden to have boyfriends while still in school, we were considered "fair game" by the opposite sex. Without boyfriends hovering around us, we were pursued, wooed, stalked, harassed, serenaded by all sorts of possible princes and obvious toads. One sweet guy sweltered in the heat of his parents' car trying to muster the courage to knock on our door and face my stern father. It took him an hour and when he finally did, the gallon of homemade ice cream that his mother made for "the girl of his dreams" had melted and was dripping through his fingers and on his shirt.

Then there were the neighborhood guys—fratmen all—who were known to be fierce *karatistas* during fraternity rumbles but who had to down bottles of San Miguel beer before they could serenade us with Filipino love songs. They would wait until the light in our room was turned off—usually around 1:00 a.m. on a Friday night—unaware that the three of us would be giggling our hearts out as we listened to them scurrying for positions outside our window. Being Cebuanos, my parents would not let us acknowledge their presence (among Tagalogs, you had to look out the window and let the serenaders in) but would allow us to peek through the curtains in the dark. None of those guys ever seriously pursued us; it appeared that they were just practicing their singing skills on us to use on the girls they really liked.

The one guy who I seriously fell for—and who eventually broke my heart—overwhelmed me with notes, letters and telegrams, sent in the most unexpected ways. Sometimes he would leave them at Vinzons Hall or tuck them in my books. Occasionally, he would ask a friend to hand one to me, or order a frat neophyte to wait outside my classroom with a bunch of roses and the missive that he (the neophyte) would be my "slave" for the day. To an innocent, self-absorbed eighteen-year-old girl, his strategy was irresistible. It certainly made the other guys look like uncreative dweebs. I mean, how could anyone's heart not melt after receiving twelve telegrams in one day, each one containing a single word that, put together, made a romantic statement proclaiming his undying affection?

At the height of all this wooing, he gave me his frat pin to wear (at that time, wearing a frat pin was a big deal) then disappeared for two weeks. When he returned, he asked for his pin back and confessed that he was forced to marry his girlfriend who was pregnant with his child!

I woke up to the realities of life and men, and shielded myself from possible hurts for years by being flaky and flighty, and avoiding those who could actually become serious suitors.

After graduation, when I got my first job with the Philippines' largest broadcasting network, I thought myself jaded and wizened, armed with the badge of an already scarred heart. Such smugness did not last. Within a day, I realized I was like Snow White entering a den of worldly, hungry lions; within a week, I understood that the local showbiz world was light years away from the innocence of campus life.

In that artificial, self-indulgent world, being married only meant that some men had to stay home on Sundays. The rest of the week they were free to have affairs, date openly, or aggressively pursue girls who struck their fancy, and those who worked with them had to accept such behavior as the natural order of things. I was in an environment unencumbered by the prevailing norms of decency and morality, and while it was a constant wild party and a lot of fun, it was a struggle to survive with one's values intact.

Being unattached and naive young girls, my friends and I were prey to the manipulative attentions of all sorts of *Pinoy* machos. And I mean all sorts. The network executives, at least, left us alone—they preferred the stars and the beauty queens who were only too eager to ensure the longevity of their careers. (In fairness, I should mention here that there were also decent, single men who led regular lives.)

My scariest experience was with this really weird guy who worked in another department and who would come to our office after he punched out at 5:00 p.m. each day. He would sit in the visitor's chair and stare at me, intensely, silently. My male friends, sensing it was a potential Maggie de la Riva situation (she was the actress who was raped by four men who were eventually executed by electric chair), would try to cajole him into joining them for drinks or after-office basketball to steer him away from me. But he would refuse. He never talked to me or even tried to accost me. But he would sit there and stare until it was time for me to go home. I was scared out of my wits but didn't know what to do.

Until my boss, a sultry, sexy woman who could play her low, radio-announcer voice as an instrument for seduction one moment and as a deadly weapon the next, decided it was time to end the madness. As the stalker took his seat one afternoon, she abruptly pulled him up by his collar, dragged him to an empty room, and obviously scared him so seriously that he never came back. Whenever we would meet him in the hallway after that, or especially when I was with my boss, who usually wore hot pants and knee-high boots, he would cower in fear and scamper away like a rat.

Now that sexual harassment has become a national issue, I long for those halcyon days when it was dealt with swiftly without the participation of lawyers and courts.

As my 18-year-old daughter prepares to go away to college, I tell her these stories with the not-so-subtle intention of sharpening her rat-detection instincts. It's a tricky job, because I have to straddle the thin line between praising men and warning her of potential frustrations. Don't repeat my mistakes, I remind her. In the next breath, I wax whimsical about the fun I had growing up being wined and wooed.

Last month, she received a present of flowers and a teddy bear from a guy who wanted her to go to the prom with him. "God, no," she exclaimed. "Why not?" I asked. "It's only one night, for god's sake, why don't you just go as friends and have fun?" But she is a child of the '90s and unequivocal about her refusals. She tossed the card into the trash can. When she wasn't looking I retrieved it and stuck it in her drawer. Someday, I'm sure, that note will amuse her, or even console her.

Some of us never learn.

•*Businessworld* Outpost, April 1999•

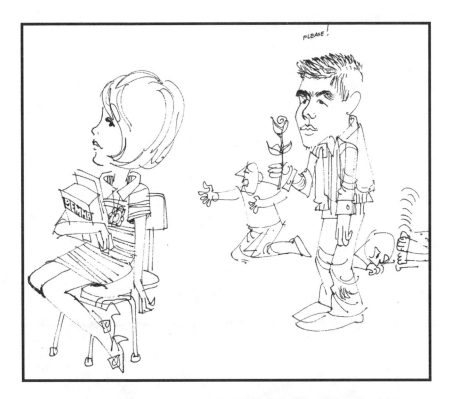

(Above) My college barkada and I would hang out at Vinzon's Hall, the student center of the University of the Philippines (UP), with Ely Santiago, who became a famous cartoonist and painter. On scraps of paper or napkins he would chronicle snippets of our lives through his sketches.

(Right) My I.D. picture at the UP.

(Above) The requisite frolicking-in-the-snow photo that new immigrants would send home to show that they're in America.

(Right) Together with two thousand others, I took my oath as a U.S. citizen on a wintry day in San Francisco in 1996.

(Below) Every kid's mecca: Disneyland. I'm so thankful I'm finally done with having to go there.

I consider Maia my singular achievement. She's the kid I raised—and shaped—on my own.

Grown up Maia and best friend Faith would sing together in school events.

The evolution of our family or how we grew up and grew stronger. When we immigrated in November 1988, Carlo was 10, Jaja was 8 and Maia was 9 months old and still learning to stand on her own. We were able to make it, albeit with great difficulty, without becoming homeless or going on welfare, thanks to my job and my in-laws.

Maia's debut in February 2006 carried on the tradition of a Filipino debut—the cotillion, the eighteen candles and roses—but without the father-daughter first dance (for obvious reasons) and with a lot less extravagance.

Carlo, Jaja and Maia in a rare display of harmony.

With Carlo (above) and Jaja (right)

The UP Alumni Association of America gave me an Outstanding Professional Award for Journalism in October 2005. In my acceptance speech I said I had to have all three of my children attend the event so they will realize there's more to their mother than the nagging and the bad cooking.

(Left) With high school classmates Benjie Dizon and Freddie Poe in Chinatown, New York

(Below) With the staff of *Filipinas Magazine*

We've Got Mail

IT's 5:30 A.M. My alarm rings obnoxiously, piercing the dark stillness and interrupting my slumber. Through most of my night-owl existence, waking up at this hour has been painful. I have never done it willingly or gracefully—not even when my babies were screaming from hunger.

These days, however, as soon as I hear the alarm, I'm awake and starting the morning stretches that my brittle back requires. That done, I go downstairs—very quietly so I don't wake up the kids—to the computer and download my email.

I hate to admit it but I have become an e-mail junkie. Ever since some forty classmates of mine from elementary and high school at the University of the Philippines reconnected in cyberspace some months ago, my life has changed. Now I claim Internet time at least twice a day, fret when I cannot use a computer, and even postpone early evening dinners because that's when some of us chat online.

My waking up at an ungodly hour each workday is a necessity. If I don't, I wouldn't have enough time to make my daughter's lunch. I get an average of twenty messages from classmates scattered across the globe. And that's just in the morning; when I get home from work, there are more. It takes more than an hour to read through them and respond to each one.

We never seem to run out of stories to tell—memories from our youth, our lives now. Each one of us has posted her *talambuhay* (short autobiography) of what we have done since we graduated from UP High. Though some had stayed in touch, many had not seen or heard from each other since the stroke of midnight that day in 1965 when we held hands and sang "Auld Lang Syne' to mark the end of our high school years and the conclusion of our graduation ball.

And what lives we have led! Mila, who was once the most wanted female guerrilla in the Philippines, with one of the biggest rewards promised for her capture, has become a devout Christian. She has been using her considerable writing abilities to promote Philippine culture and, in our listserv, to explain the Word to classmates like me, whose religious inclinations are tenuous at best.

Several classmates in the Midwest and the South, and in Canada are information technology specialists, riding high in this time of high-tech skills shortage. We have lawyers in the group and doctors of varied specialties. Ray, who was among the most mischievous in our batch, is now a pediatrician in the Northeast. He hardly has time to write messages but when he does, we all die laughing—to the consternation of our children, who think us "weird" for chuckling in the dark.

And Tony E., the "rug-cutter of the year" of the Class of '65, who I haven't seen since he played in the University of the Philippines (UP) Varsity basketball team in college, is as funny as ever, especially in his unabashed amazement at how the shy, introverted girls he used to tease in high school have turned into strong, lusty women, unapologetic for their sensuality.

There's Tony P., who is the CEO of a beverage firm back home; Steve, our group moderator, who is a lawyer and real-estate developer; the glamour girls who have become successful businesswomen; Noel, who is a well-known tenor honed in the classics, and Becky, who sings revolutionary songs; and Chit, the physics instructor at UP who is now a manager of a giant telecommunications firm. We just found out that Jeffty, another of our class jesters, actually became her student and would cut classes and cheat during exams. Yet she gave him a passing grade.

After months of daily conversations and revelations of long-held secrets, of sharing each other's woes and even praying together in cyberspace, we continue to be amazed at how we, the class who came of age at the dawn of the fractious '70s, have managed to come together after decades of disconnection and effortlessly picked up from where we left off.

Is it because we grew up together, like brothers and sisters, when we were still diamonds in the rough? Someone said we couldn't help but be honest now because after all, we knew each other before we donned the many masks of adulthood.

Being in the vicinity of the big 5-0 must have something to do with it, too. Like our fellow boomers, we are torn between free-spiritedness and responsibility. We crave to get off the career track and live it up as retirees, even as we still have children to support and reputations to uphold. Like the adolescents that we once were—and in many ways, still are—we ignore our mortality. We once joked about getting together in some beach house somewhere when we are in our eighties, to smoke pot and drink pitchers of margarita, because then we would no longer be required to be good citizens.

However one may explain this "cyber *barangay*" of ours, it has done wonders for our psyche and our health. Not only do we share techniques for relieving our aching backs and taming our menopausal mood swings, we are also a support group to those going through difficult life situations. Better than Prozac, as one gleefully puts it.

This month, after thirty-four years of going our separate ways, we are having a reunion in the Bay Area. It's far from where we started from but, geographic details aside, the UP High Class of '65 is coming home to each other at last.

•*Filipinas* Magazine, April 1999•

Romantic Fugue

THEY FOUND each other when they were still trying to find themselves. Their friends had been eager to manufacture a romance to gossip about and they were the chosen ones. Unlike the tales of first love in literature, there was no lightning and thunder that accompanied their introduction, no clanging of bells or orchestral fugue to mark the moment. He was, in fact, initially turned off by her reserve; it seemed like she was lost in her own world and he was an intruder.

It was easy to wipe out that initial impression. The more time they spent together, the more they discovered they had much in common. If they only knew what soul mates were then, they would have defined themselves as such. He remembers their long conversations that would start when they met each morning and ended late at night over the phone. He knew everything there was to know about her, he thought. He could anticipate what delighted her, her moods, the things that made her laugh. She knew him just as thoroughly, except that what they told each other was just what they knew of themselves. At their age, that wasn't much.

He did not see the break coming. One night, as they were watching the stars come out, he asked her if she had ever imagined how their children would look like. He felt her tense slightly but didn't think much of it because she merrily evaded the question by bringing up another topic.

He did not push the issue; it was, after all, idle talk, and he was afraid that if she threw the same question at him, he wouldn't know what to say.

Each of them became busy trying to carve out their niches in different fields. Although they were still a couple and they still had those long phone conversations, their new jobs did not allow them to be with each other as much. The diminished time together did not bother him. He was, in fact, enjoying being on his own, as an individual rather than the other half of a couple. He had no doubt that they would someday marry. And when she told him she was leaving, he considered it a temporary separation and did not grieve. But she knew better.

Each morning when the phone rang, she knew exactly what time it was and who was calling. There was something quite endearing in his insistence on this routine. It was almost as if he needed the predictability to assuage his fear of her unpredictability. Poor guy, he never really understood what it was that drove her away at that time when their world was wrapped around each other. She herself couldn't define it then. She felt the intensity of her restlessness and the need to be free but didn't yet have the words that could make him understand. And so she left him with weak reasons and empty promises, though she knew deep inside her that she was not going back.

She did not try to find out how he felt when he realized the finality of her leaving. That was almost three decades ago so she saw no point in dredging up dormant emotions.

They found each other again when he bumped into an old friend who had her current phone number. When he called, she realized she didn't know much about him other than that he had married and had been successful. She thought their first meeting would be awkward but no, it turned out to be very pleasant. Like the old friends that they were, they picked up where they left off so smoothly, it was almost like their wrinkles and gray hairs were just affectations they had put on to amuse each other. But those were just the externals.

They learned soon enough how different each had become. He had acquired the trappings of a traditional life but there was an emptiness in his soul that he never quite understood, so he kept it buried—until he met their common friend and, without his planning to, asked about her.

For her part, she consciously lived her life in phases; each phase as different from the previous ones as she could make it. She told him her story as plainly as she could but she could see that he was alternately perplexed and fascinated by the tangled web she had created for herself and how unapologetic she was of her choices and her follies. This is me, she stressed, I am no longer eighteen and I have my scars to show for it.

It is never easy to rekindle a romance from the ashes of years, but they managed. Scratch that. A better way to put it is: It is quite a feat to start a romance when the two individuals involved have a past to get over and the baggage of years to shed before they could truly be together. But they did it. They are in love again, but this time without that cloying togetherness that suffocated them in the past. They see each other when they want to, allowing each other the space they need to continue growing.

Will they live happily ever after? They don't know. Nobody knows. In love and in life, there are no guarantees. But in the game of chance, this couple has so much going for them. They have, after all, paid their dues and have come out winning.

•*Filipinas* Magazine, February 2001•

Grieving

How do we speak of grief? We draw on our usual arsenal of words: ache, longing, pain, suffering, anguish, sorrow, heartbreak. Pile on some adjectives: heavy, unbearable, intense, devastating, constant. But somehow when we are going through our personal hells, these words sound hollow and inadequate. They don't describe the dread we feel when the sun is disappearing in the horizon, the darkness is setting in, and we have to negotiate the night alone, unable and unwilling to sleep because the momentary respite only leads to a more vigorous ache in the heart the next morning.

No, these words do not even come close to describing how our days are shrouded in gray because the sunshine is gone from our lives, and we move around like a robot, stiff and unfeeling, since our broken hearts have sapped our senses of every sensation and snuffed out the light in our eyes.

How do we explain the way our hearts constrict when we absentmindedly turn to share a quip, a bit of news, an opinion, and then we realize that the person we wanted to share it with is no longer around? Is there a way to convey the full measure of interrupted lives, lost dreams, and shattered illusions?

When Omar, a person I had a lot of affection for, was killed in the vilest possible manner many years ago, I plunged into a sadness so deep, it took me a very long time before I could climb out of it. In the months following his death, I was a wreck. My days were filled with tears and exhaustion, my nights with nightmares and loneliness.

Those who have experienced such grief recognize the helplessness one feels when one's life is spinning out-of-control. One cries at the most inopportune moments, each time one remembers the face and one's loss, which is very often; and at night, one goes down on one's knees and pray fervently for just a few minutes together so one can say a proper farewell.

Eventually—because one has to—one learns to build up one's defenses and carve out a new life from the debris of the previous one, but there will always be an empty space within that can never be filled even by the happiness one may later manage to achieve.

It has been almost thirty years since I lost Omar but not a week goes by without my thinking of him. The pain is dulled now, even his face has become blurry, but through all of my tragedies and triumphs—through the sheer joy of having my children, for example —I would always wonder how my life would be if he were still around.

Carrying his memory like a secret *anting-anting* (talisman) had become second nature to me. I have become so good at hiding this ache, that hardly anyone among the people I have met after his death even knows about it. But when a few months ago, his brother (whom I was meeting for the first time) suggested that we let him go, to finally rest in peace, I could not do so willingly. I was afraid that if I let go he would be gone from my consciousness forever and I could not accept that. Then I woke up one morning, on the day he would have turned fifty, feeling lighter and freer. I couldn't really articulate what brought about the change, but somehow I had an epiphany, that by letting go of my sadness he would become a happier presence in my life.

That morning, I bought some flowers and laid them at the edge of the bay so the waves could pull them from the shore. I stood there for a long time, watching the flowers float away until they were just tiny specks in the horizon. I was saying goodbye to my grief and acknowledging that I will now see my friend in every blade of grass, in every blooming flower, in everything that is beautiful in this world.

I am sharing these very private thoughts today because the past few months have brought too many losses and tragedies. It is so easy, tempting even, to wallow in despair and bitterness. While there should be time for these, the bigger challenge—and the sweeter triumph—is in barreling into the sunshine despite the clouds that have wrapped around us, like skin. Easier said than done, I know. It took me twenty-eight years to figure this out.

How can we speak of redemption? We may use such words as recovery, regeneration, rebirth, salvation, but they cannot capture the music in our soul as we emerge from the thicket of our agony. It may be a slow process, and oftentimes we may feel guilty because it will seem like we have forgotten. But moving on is not forgetting. We just learn to shed our sadness over the end of a significant phase of our life and instead rejoice that it happened.

November begins in our homeland with a festive commemoration of the dead and ends in our adopted country with a celebration of thanksgiving. There is a lesson there that we should take to heart.

•*Filipinas* Magazine, November 2001•

Basking In the Afterglow

IT's BEYOND midnight—way past my usual bedtime—but sleep eludes me and I am swinging from restlessness to weariness, muscles aching, eyes smarting. I check my e-mail constantly, knowing that in other parts of the country some of my friends are likewise going through this edginess that comes with having to come back down to earth from three days of an adrenaline high.

No, I am not addicted to anything even if I do exhibit the symptoms of withdrawal. Nor am I having a clandestine affair and suffering the torment of separation (in which case I wouldn't be writing about it.)

I just got back from the UP High School Class of '65 Reunion in New York, our second big one in two years, and I tell you, the entire event was so rejuvenating, it was painful to see it end.

Among the UP High batches, ours is probably one of the most active in getting together. We've had mini-reunions in Manila sporadically since we finished college, drawing a crowd of around fifteen each time. But those early get-togethers, though fun, had a patina of discomfort to them. We were still charting our directions and were not quite there yet. We were still trying to shake off our adolescent personality defects along with whatever lingering hurts some had inflicted on others.

But beneath the posturing then, there was always a strong bond among us who spent seven hours of each school day for four years together.

Though we could only claim a few classmates as friends (many of us never even exchanged a word with each other in high school), somehow the shared experience of teenage foibles and growing up in the mid-'60s, when the Beatles were breaking all the musical rules but our parents and teachers still lived by strict ordinances that managed to suppress our raging hormones, gave us a common—and unbreakable—lifeline to which we have held on, very often unconsciously, through our adulthood, marriage, parenthood and for some, even divorce.

When one of us was in trouble (as in being imprisoned under martial law), we got together to help in whatever way we could. When some were going through their personal hells, there would be classmates to hold their hands and get them through the bad nights.

The boys, it turned out, established more enduring friendships, bound as they were by the pranks and the risks they took in their journey to manhood. When they told us their stories, we girls were wide-eyed with amazement that those shy, bumbling dweebs were actually having the time of their lives like only teenage boys could. We were totally clueless then.

But for these occasional gatherings, we lived mostly separate lives for more than thirty years—until e-mail happened and we got reconnected. No longer stymied by our adolescent fears (heck, we can't even remember them anymore), we started bonding as mellowed, battle-scarred adults. Through the safe distance and the virtual intimacy of cyberspace, we shared our life stories and got to know each other as individuals for the first time through the conversations and the jokes that we posted daily, sometimes reaching one hundred messages a day.

When we decided to get together for a grand reunion in the San Francisco Bay Area last year, it was an effortless progression toward the renewal of our bond that had tightened considerably in cyberspace. We no longer met as strangers—e-mail had eliminated the initial awkwardness—and it just felt so right to come together and actually hug and kiss like members of one big, noisy, rowdy family. That reunion snagged fifty classmates (out of a batch of 130 or so) who flew in from Manila, Hong Kong, Singapore and many parts of the United States.

And it was just the beginning. In the intervening months between San Francisco and New York, our class has had mini-reunions whenever someone came to visit and each time, more and more of the batch joined in. Our listserv, which started out with about thirty people, now has more than eighty members and there are still many of our classmates who are in constant touch with others who do not have e-mail. Even some of our UP Elementary School classmates who did not go to UP High have been integrated into the group that we often forget that they were not actually part of class '65.

Unlike the San Francisco reunion which was driven by the thrill of anticipation (How do they look now? How will I look to them?), this year's New York event was more of a homecoming. Though there were "new" attendees who had just been "found," many of us had met previously and were picking up from were we left off last year. It was like an annual retreat where for three full days we set aside our daily stresses and reconnected with that part of us that will always be young and free and unequivocally happy.

It was a rejuvenation that we all needed and we promised each other that we would do this every year until we are too old, or dead. But don't count on that happening anytime soon because each time we get together we invariably shave a few years off.

•*Filipinas* Magazine, July 2000.•

To a Dying Friend

Dearest J,

I can never figure this out—how does God or whoever it is that makes decisions such as this, decide which person should get sick, who should die immediately, and who should continue living? Is it just the luck of the draw that you're there right now awaiting the inevitability of your passing while I'm here still dealing with the minutiae of surviving? Why you, of all people, when you have lived a life dedicated to making this world a better place?

I could easily name ten people who should be in your place right now, whose passing will make this world safer and happier, yet there they are, in the peak of health, still strutting in the illusion of their invincibility while you are lying there wasting away, unable to finish all that you wanted to do.

Is this what Divine Justice is about or did you, in one of your adventurous treks, make the mistake of displeasing one minor god who then marked you with the insignia of death?

I can just see you now, shaking your head and smiling that magnanimous smile of yours. There you go again, you would tell me, pondering the imponderables instead of just believing and accepting. That has always been your way of tempering my rages, no matter how justified, and because you would say it with such conviction, I would calm down. And in my calm I would arrive at a solution.

You have always been wiser than me, I have always deferred to your good sense and the clarity of your reasoning. So why are you there, immobile, unspeaking when I am bent out of shape by anger, sadness, and disbelief? You always helped me get through situations like this; you promised me you would always stand by me. So why are you abandoning me now?

I'm sorry, this is so selfish and inconsiderate of me, this flailing about in all directions. So typical of me, you would say, when I am confronted with something that I can't understand and can't control. Okay, stop shaking your head; I'm simmering down now. Believe and accept. Believe and accept. Believe what? Accept what?

I wonder how you are feeling, whether you are still feeling something. When your system shuts down, does it mean all sensations are gone? What about your emotions, do they go away too? C'mon, J, you have always been generous with your knowledge, wake up and tell us how it feels to be dying. Is it true that you can see your entire life pass before you like a video on fast-forward? Or does death happen incrementally, the tips of your toes first then creeping up slowly like when you're standing in the bathtub and the water starts going up your legs?

Is "life" a feeling, a sensation that ebbs, or is it like artificial light that is gone at the flick of a switch?

I remember when I was eight years old and very sick with nephritis, I asked my father how a person would feel if he were dying. The question caught him by surprise and for once my scientist-father did not seem to know the answer although he eventually mumbled something like "an extreme tiredness." It was only years later that I realized how scared he must have been by that question since at that time, my ailment was so severe that it was touch and go for a while. Throughout the three months that I was confined to that hospital bed, I was watching out for "extreme tiredness," but of course I never found out how that felt.

Is that what's happening to you now? Did you will your body to shut down so you no longer have to deal with your pain?

Remember how we used to talk about the best way to die? You always opted for a quick way like a plane crash or a stray bullet to your brain. No time for pain or regret, you insisted. I have always opted for the chance to document the entire process; you know, a slow glamorous going, like that woman in *Love Story*, where you don't have to wither. I would write a daily diary and tell everyone who matters in my life how important they are to me.

How naïve I was, how little I knew about terminal ailments! And how arrogant to think that I could have my way in life and in death.

I am listening to the clock ticking each second to oblivion. Time has assumed a different dimension now as we wait. I close my eyes tight so I can listen to the sounds of living—there's a bird chirping and a slight breeze is making the leaves rustle. Elsewhere, I hear a neighbor's radio turned up while a car revs up its engine. Around me the computer hums its constant rhythm and my clicking of the keys seems almost musical. I've never noticed these things before, these pieces of evidence that life goes on. I wonder if in your last days of consciousness you were able to soak in the sights, the smells, the sounds, and the tastes of life. And I wonder how it felt to let go.

I guess the time has come for me to let go of you, too. This is not how it is supposed to be. We were going to grow old together so we could find out which lover we would remember when the rest of our memory had turned to mush. And now you leave me without answering that question. How fair is that?

So long, dear friend. I love you. It has been one great ride. But you still owe me an answer. And because of that, you will always, always be alive in me.

•*Filipinas* Magazine, August 2002•

Karaokay!

THERE WE WERE, a not-too-small gathering of friends (fifteen people), on a perfect Bay Area summer afternoon (sunny and a little windy, too cold for sunbathing but too enticing to spend indoors). The party was over, the food table cleared, the photos taken, but we still could not let go of each other. There was, after all, an entire evening before us and we were taking a very welcome break from our daily routines. What do we do next?

Going home and watching a ballgame on TV was not an option. That's regular weekend fare and this was an unusual day. Mahjong was out, it would break up the group; ballroom dancing was nixed, too threatening. That left us with only one choice—and it was everyone's first choice it turned out: singing. We all drove over to our neighborhood Filipino restaurant, ordered *pancit palabok, lomi, sinigang, sitsarong bulaklak* and beer, and dug in for the night.

It was one of those typical Pinoy occasions that expats like us cherish: One that lasted for hours, disregarded caution about calories and cholesterol, and salved the gaping wound that homesickness had dealt our hearts. And then, of course, there was karaoke.

It is a Filipino invention like it ought to be (although the word comes from the Japanese, who then marketed the equipment). We know how musical we are as a nation and how important singing is to our collective soul. The troubadours of Asia, Filipino performers are called. Singing, to us, is what percussion is to Africans and mambo is to the Latin Americans. It is elemental to our existence. We don't just sing in the shower, we carry a song in us wherever we may be—in the subway, at work, at play, when we're happy or sad, when praying or making love.

Notice how spontaneously we pick up a tune even if we're doing something totally unrelated, like choosing vegetables at the supermarket or rushing into a crowded elevator. We hear Frank Sinatra crooning "... and there were times/I'm sure you knew/when I bit off more than I could chew ..." and we sing the entire song, even if just in our heads. When Mick Jagger screams "I can't get no ... satisfaction" we add some rhythm and spring to our steps.

Between the two Filipino proclivities—karaoke singing and ballroom dancing—I think karaoke wins, at least in the Bay Area. Without a karaoke, a restaurant will find it difficult to compete for the Filipino market, according to someone who used to manage one. To prove his point, there are three Filipino restaurants within five miles from our house and all of them have karaoke nights that draw quite a crowd. Karaoke joints are like the beer gardens back home—places to relax in when the day has been tough, except you don't get *inihaw na pusit* (grilled squid) for *pulutan* nor will a waiter leave a plastic case beside you for the beer bottles you have emptied.

Karaoke, however, is more than just a good business strategy. It is a transformative experience. Notice how the shy ones in the group start out by refusing to sing because they are self-conscious about the quality of their voices or their ability to carry a tune. And then as the night wears on and the gaiety level rises (in many instances, in proportion to the intoxication level), their inhibition starts dissipating and pretty soon, they're singing the night away just like everyone else. I've been wondering, is it the music or the microphone that transforms people?

I must admit it took me a while to appreciate karaoke. I'm a child of the '60s, who still clings to wonderful memories of singing groups and acoustic guitars. On lazy Sunday afternoons then, when the summers were too hot for us to stay inside the house, my cousins and I would bring a case of Sarsi to our porch, along with a big can of La Pacita biscuits and a bucket of ice. Then we would start singing the few songs we knew how to play on the guitar. They were the easy ones: the Beatles' "Follow the Sun" and "'Til There Was You," the Everly Brothers' "Devoted to You," and "Where Have All the Flowers Gone" by Peter, Paul and Mary. Pretty soon our neighbors, who were better guitar players, would come for the company and the merienda and we would inevitably end up as a big group singing together, no microphones or soloists, every voice finding its way to contribute to the harmony.

Because of these memories, I always considered karaoke crass and undemocratic. One person holds the mike and imposes his/her singing on everyone else. If we're lucky, that person can be a good singer or is mercifully generous with sharing the microphone. There's always a fifty-fifty chance that we'll end up as mere bystanders in an agonizing evening of bad singing.

But one day a friend came by brandishing his magic mic like a fairy godmother's wand. Try it just once, he urged. I held the microphone and felt a tingling in my nerves as the first strains of my song started playing and the words were projected on the TV screen. I was safe in my living room and I've always said, I'm willing to try anything once. After a few seconds of hesitation, I plunged right into the music, the video, the entire karaoke experience.

And I have not been the same since.

•*Filipinas* Magazine, September 2002•

Girlfriends

IT'S FOUR in the morning—an hour that almost always finds us sleeping—but here we are, a group of wide-awake middle-aged women merrily chatting and giggling the way our daughters do when they have their sleepovers, the way we did when we were much younger and more energetic. This time it is different. We are in New York, in a hotel room, each of us taking a very welcome and well-deserved break from our humdrum lives back home, all of us fifty-something women with dyed hair, expanding waistlines and hot flashes to show for it.

Those who make it a point to spend time with girlfriends know how incredibly invigorating it can be. Like tripping without the acid, orgasms without the chest thumping, liberation without the anger. Okay, maybe I'm stretching my hyperboles here but you get my drift. Girlfriends, meaning those who are real friends, are necessary for our sanity. They fill up those empty spaces in our souls that our male partners cannot fill, no matter how well they try, simply because they are not, well, women.

Our partners may take us to Keanu Reeves' latest movie, knowing that we like him, and we are grateful for their thoughtfulness. But girlfriends are the ones who understand (even without our articulating it) that we watch Keanu not for his screen presence and his acting but because when he smiles, he reminds us of that one guy who got away but who still elicits pleasant sensations within us. Men (and our children) will find it gross or threatening that we entertain such fantasies. But soul sisters know instinctively that we clutch at whatever straws we can to carve a passionate life out of the parameters we have willingly or unwittingly adopted to define our existence.

Soul sisters however can be hard to find. There are no instruction manuals, no Help menus to guide us through the necessary process of extricating chaff from grain. Often it takes years of closeness, quarrels, and separations before we can zero in on those we can trust with our deepest secrets. A lot of times, those who we thought are our sisters of the heart turn out to be snakes.

It's just like searching for the perfect mate—we pick up heartaches and betrayals along the way. Unlike searching for a perfect mate, however, we don't settle for the "next best thing" when it comes to girlfriends because there is no biological clock ticking, no overriding compulsion to share a life with them. It could take a lifetime to find our sisters of choice. But if we're lucky, it shouldn't take that long.

I consider myself fortunate to have found women friends I can laugh and cry with without being judged. And therein lies the gist of girlfriendhood: We may criticize and scold each other, be brutally frank about our flaws, but at the end of the day (or a fight) we know that we have no other agenda but to be present for each other in whatever circumstance we may find ourselves in. We are each other's therapists and safe havens, and heaven knows how much we need that kind of reassurance as we play the cards that life has dealt us.

I am particularly appreciative of my closest girlfriends because I am once again at a crossroad, a situation that lends itself to great opportunities and gigantic mistakes. Fifteen years ago, my women writer-friends in Manila rode the treacherous waves with me as I negotiated the end of my marriage and my move to the U.S., with three small children in tow. While my male friends did all they could to ease the transition, it was my women friends who brought solace to my pain, making me laugh through my tears, going with me to do silly things like consulting all the seers, astrologers, and fortune-tellers we could find just to reassure myself that I was making the right decision.

This time around it is my high school classmates—people I grew up with but never really got close to until recently when we were finally able to connect with each other without being threatened by our juvenile insecurities—who are holding my hand as I ride my current roller coaster. Though they may not always agree with my choices, they celebrate with me my joys and embrace me through my sorrows. They make themselves available to me 24/7 as I do to them. Since we are no longer encumbered by growing children who require constant one-on-one attention, we are freer to meet up when someone has to unburden. On several occasions, we have summoned each other when we needed to cry over something, for whatever crazy reason it might be.

Just like tonight, in this hotel room in New York, where we are talking, laughing, and crying while trying out new outfits we have shopped for earlier in the day. We live for togetherness such as this because it revives us, recharges our batteries, and gives us the ammunition we need to face the life battles—those inevitable and endless trials that lie in wait for us to tackle.

•*Filipinas* Magazine, September 2003•

the philippines
is in the heart

Rainy Days and Fun Days

WHEN WE HEAR the rain falling steadily on our rooftops and watch it cascade down our windows, we witness the way plants and grass seem to bloom before our eyes in celebration and feel a deep and unshakeable longing for those things that held us together back home when the rains fell in torrents for weeks at a time, and the world as we knew it seemed to have stopped in its tracks.

This is how I'm feeling right now, as I write this piece, amidst a rainstorm that is puny compared to what we Filipinos know rainstorms to be. Outside, the traffic is a mess and people must be cold to their bones in this freezing rain of winter. No matter. I banish real-world concerns from my thoughts as I snuggle in the warmth of a blanket and a cup of piping hot chocolate.

When I was growing up in the University of the Philippines campus, the coming of the monsoon rains brought squeals of delight because it meant we no longer had to swelter in the humidity and we could run outside and let the cool raindrops soak us to the skin. Those were the days before acid rain, when our elders were only too willing to let us go out and play because it was supposed to heal the prickly heat rash that made us itch at night.

Rain was liberating. Not only was it water play, it allowed us to sink our bare feet into the soil that was previously forbiddingly dry. We remember the intensity of the pleasure of the still-warm ground giving way to our soles as it slowly turns to gooey mud. There were puddles to jump over, wet bermuda grass that ceased to prick, yellow bells we could fill with raindrops then pop like little balloons, its shattered petals sticking to our wet clothes like confetti. Best of all, there were no adults to stop us from indulging our thrills. They never knew that we would chuck our slippers as soon as we were out of their sight and wade in dirty water, totally forgetting the fear of ringworms that they had instilled in us.

When we had our fill of sloshing and romping, when our teeth started chattering from the cold that seeped into our bones, we would go home to a warm bath and hot soup, and be lulled to sleep by the sound of rain dribbling on our rooftops.

The next day we considered ourselves lucky if it would still be raining hard because that meant school would be suspended and we could again go out and play. Only much later did we come to understand the inconvenience, even the destruction that monsoon rains could cause. Somehow we were unmindful of the buckets that had to be brought out to catch the leaks from the roofs of our quonset huts. Our school building, a remnant of the Second World War, would flood in places and soak some of our teachers' materials in putrid water that seeped through the *sawali* walls.

And there were the thunderstorms. They started as faint flashes of light and distant rumbles but they would inevitably get closer and louder until the lightning and thunder would happen at the same time, so close to our houses that we would hide in the closets and plug our ears tight with our fingers. There are no real thunderstorms here where I live now and somehow—crazy as this may sound—I miss them.

I miss running for cover as light and sound collided. I miss the fear that heaven's wrath was upon us (as the adults would warn) and our childish innocence that made us accept such threats without questioning. If the thunderstorm was particularly severe, a blackout would occur and we would play hide-and-seek in the dark or listen as the adults told us scary stories.

I miss those simple pleasures that too easily morphed into grown-up disenchantment. We learned too soon the scientific explanation for thunderstorms and the disruptiveness of monsoon rains and we lost our spontaneous ability to be awed. Instead, we grumbled about inconsequential things like mud in our shoes and the mosquitoes that invariably appeared after a rain.

One particularly difficult year, it rained continuously night and day for more than a month, creating deep potholes in the streets and making travel very difficult. Events were cancelled, life in the city almost ground to a halt and people began to feel that the deluge was God's punishment for the decadence of the times.

The typhoons became increasingly ferocious. One completely blew off our roof and destroyed our campus cottage so we had to spend the night at the Faculty Center without electricity or water, and only a few dry clothes to keep us from getting sick. Although that was depressing, I look back to it now with fondness because we were with friends and we spent the night singing and telling stories by candlelight and sharing the few cigarettes that someone managed to salvage from soggy packs. It was one of the most heartwarming nights I've ever spent.

Some of those friends are gone now, their lives snuffed out tragically and too soon. I long for them in moments like this when it is dark, cold and rainy, and I am thousands of miles away from the storms that once stoked the fire in my soul.

•*Filipinas* Magazine, January 2001•
Originally titled "Rain and Remembrance"

Infidelity

JOINING THE waiting crowd at a car wash one weekend morning, I gravitated toward a group of Filipinas of varying ages who were obviously having a good time. They were chatting like old friends even if, I found out later, they did not know each other until then. The topic that triggered so much mirth was these four ladies' common search for a worthy partner, a goal that had not yet been achieved but the pursuit of which had yielded fodder not only for good conversation but a novel perhaps, or at the very least, a comedy routine.

"*Basta ako*," the more assertive lady stated, "I keep away from Filipino men." "*Bakit naman?*" I queried, genuinely surprised that this woman who seemed deeply rooted in Filipino culture would make such a definitive statement, which, by the way, elicited nods of approval from the two younger women who were newcomers to the U.S. "*Eh kasi, aalilain ka na, kakaliwain ka pa.*" (Not only will they treat you like a servant, they will be unfaithful.)

When I told some of my male friends about this incident, only one actually laughed; another one said it was unfair but understood where the women were coming from; the rest made some snide remarks about how the ladies must have looked and that maybe Filipino men, in their infinite good taste, would never look in their direction.

The Filipino male's reputation for adultery is perhaps undeserved, but only to a certain extent. Certainly not all Filipino men are unfaithful; many others would claim to be faithful although they may falter when asked to define fidelity. Some say they are faithful because they do not ever look at another woman with lust—which only means they are either blind, dead or lying. Others do a Clintonesque contortion: They are not unfaithful for as long as they don't get emotionally involved with another woman, a statement that has truly disturbing implications because it suggests that it's okay to use a woman as an object for sexual gratification for as long as she remains just that—an object.

However one defines infidelity, there is no denying that a lot of Filipino males, especially those who are living in the Philippines, are unfaithful to their partners. I used to think that it was largely a matter of economics or stature: The more financially comfortable or powerful a man is, the greater his tendency to stray, like it is some perk that comes with success. But I have realized that infidelity transcends economic or social status. We were once on a bus to Northern Luzon which took longer than usual at a pit stop in some town. Impatient at the long wait, we started looking for the driver but we were hushed when some folks told us that he was visiting his mistress with whom he had several children. Ooo-kay.

Going through my own experience with infidelity, I was shocked at how accepting Philippine society was of men who strayed. (Look at how President Estrada is totally unapologetic about his having one true wife and four, or is it five, mistresses.) I mean I was getting comments like "Maybe it's your fault," or "He's just being a male" or worse, "Just wait it out, he'll come back to you because you're his wife," as if a marriage is a basketball game with fouls and time-outs. And those statements came from women!

Despite that sad episode (which I resolved by ending the marriage which was, for the most part, already dead)—and maybe because I have gotten over it completely—I cannot bring myself to totally condemn the faithless men I know. I don't condone their actions, nor will I agree to cover for them while they gallivant. But somehow I retain some sympathy for them (mixed with a bit of condescension, I must admit) because they are so naïve.

Shielded by Philippine society's seeming acceptance of their shenanigans, they think they can have the best of both worlds: An intact family that they can be with on weekends and fun with their girlfriends on weekdays. They are almost always unprepared for the tsunami that hits them when their wives fight back, their families dissolve, their children refuse to talk to them and their friends abandon them.

And Filipina wives, weary of marital neglect, are fighting back in various ways. While the law still prohibits the dissolution of a marriage—there is still no divorce in the Philippines—wives are breaking from the traditional cultural mold that they are boxed into and are seeking support from friends and professionals, pursuing their own interests (like ballroom dancing) and opening up separate realities for themselves outside of their husbands' spheres.

Which probably adds fodder to a wayward husband's usual line to a girlfriend that goes something like, "My wife and I no longer have a relationship but I cannot leave her because of the children. I need you." Oh, puh-leeze. Isn't there a more original cop-out line?

•*Filipinas* Magazine, June 2000•
Originally titled "Astray in the Fields of the Lord"

May, Come She Will

SOMETHING ABOUT May. Even here in the San Francisco Bay Area, where the temperature is nippy and the air is swirling with allergens, the sun seems to shine brighter, the aroma of the breeze sweeter and the colors of the world more intense. The wildflowers are everywhere even in the most unexpected places, defying logic by sprouting from solid rock, making entire hills appear covered with gold. In May. So much beauty around us if we only take the time to stop and look.

For those who have spent part of their lives in the Philippines, May is similarly a month a flowers and sunshine. When I was a child, I would spend part of afternoons with my friends stringing garlands of *kalachuchi* and *sampaguita*, or arranging bouquets out of the many blooms in the gardens. Then my friends and I would walk to church for the daily service called *Flores de Mayo* that involved saying the rosary and some prayers to the Virgin Mary before lining up to offer our individual floral creations. While the priest would often remind us that any offering will do, that even a blade of grass is welcome, we would always try for the best combination of colors and scents, not just to honor the Virgin Mary but to titillate our senses.

In my young heart, nothing was more satisfying than to press my nose on a colorful bouquet of subtle fragrances.

There was one time when my friends and I dared go beyond the yellow bells, the red *gumamela*, and the *violetas* that were always within our reach, and aspired for the fiery orange blossoms of the *caballero* trees that lined the streets. Those were old trees, see, and in their full glory, they formed a canopy that was an explosion of color so intense, we could only compare it to fire. Like moths to the flame, we were drawn to them despite the warnings of the adults and the danger posed by the buses that plied that route.

The day when we just had to have some of those flowers for *Flores de Mayo*, we went as a group. One guy who was older and bigger than most of us was in charge of climbing a tree and cutting off the branches that had the most blossoms. Others brought long poles to prod the more fragile stems to break. The rest of us were in charge of catching the falling flowers. A fine enough arrangement except that we did not realize until it was too late that the fire trees were laden with *higad*, those tiny, furry worms that hang on branches and make any human who came in contact with even just one, itch like crazy. By the time we got our flowers, all of us were scratching and swollen. I don't remember if anyone made it to *Flores de Mayo* that afternoon; I'm not even sure if we managed to bring our hard-earned loot home. It was an early lesson for us that so much beauty could also bring so much misery.

May back home is also the month of the *Santacruzan*, an elaborate procession that has been transformed in the past decades into a showcase of wealth, a fashion show for aspiring couturiers, and a beauty pageant, all in one. In many instances, the religious intent is overshadowed by the secular ostentation, something that I always thought the Catholic Church should object to, except that such displays of extravagance must also mean a proportional increase in its coffers.

To those of us with provincial roots, this month always brings nostalgia for the fiesta. A number of important saints—notably San Isidro, the patron saint of farmers—have their feast days in May, making many normally sleepy towns explode in once-a-year revelry. A town fiesta is enough reason to go home, not just for those who have moved to different areas in the Philippines but for expats and tourists who want to witness Philippine culture at its most colorful and most hospitable.

A fiesta is a feast to the senses. There are church bells pealing at various times, loudspeakers blaring music, peddlers yelling, raucous public dances in the plaza, stage shows featuring aspiring local singers and comedy skits by midgets, cockfights and the accompanying roar of the crowd, ferris wheels and mini roller coasters eliciting screams, and booths featuring various strange games that involve oddball elements such as white mice and spiders. Because May is the height of summer, there are vendors selling juices and ice cream of various tastes and hues, scooped into glasses dipped in a basin of already foggy water.

Then, of course, there is the food. At a Philippine fiesta, no one is a stranger. Everyone is expected to go to each house, even of strangers, to partake of the fare the hosts spent a year saving for. It would be rude not to eat and rudeness is unacceptable, where townsfolk and visitors alike let down their decorum and reserve, and allow themselves to be swept into the Bacchanalian celebration.

For former residents going home to visit, the fiesta is like a spiritual retreat, a time for grounding. No matter how far they have gone from their former lives, there is always the thrill of linking up with those who stayed behind and returning to the rituals that once bound them together. I have always been envious of how my brother and sister could slip so naturally into the slow beat of life in our father's hometown and start conversations with their old friends like the interruption happened only yesterday, not decades before. Since I've never spent more than a week there, I was always the semi-stranger who was treated royally but could never share the nuances of life in the town.

Yet when May comes around, I always find myself looking back with fondness to the fiestas in our home town, and the other towns I've been to, knowing deep in my heart that when the time comes for me to embrace a quiet life, those are the places I will return to and finally call my home.

•*Filipinas* Magazine, May 2003•

Victual Reality

MAIA, WHO has spent most of her life in California, grimaced as she watched Carlo, Jaja and I load our mango slices with *bagoong* (shrimp paste). "Eeuww, it's that stinky stuff again," she complained.

This was not the first time an ocean of difference divided our bi-cultural, multi-generational household. First of all, there were those moments when I was tempted to flagellate myself for having raised independent-minded, assertive kids who felt free to contradict me like they knew everything. (God, they can be exasperating!) The issue of food, however, simmered beneath the otherwise genuine confluence of tastes, attitudes, and outlook that the children and I have managed to establish for the most part.

First there is *adobo*. More than any other dish, this is my comfort food. There's nothing like the aroma of vinegar and garlic over hot oil to prod me out of my doldrums. It doesn't matter if it's just chicken or pork, or a mix of both; for as long as it is cooked with an entire head of crushed garlic, *sukang paombong* (native vinegar), and peppercorns, that's my *adobo*. And then of course, when it's done and I have scooped out the meat from the pan, I fry rice in the remaining sauce so that there is not a single drop wasted. "You never wash the pan after cooking *adobo*," I tell anyone who cares to listen.

Maia loves the dish; Carlo and Jaja, my two very Filipino older kids, don't (although they will eat *sinangag* anytime). "Where did I go wrong with you guys?" I ask, repeating my mantra. "You must have screwed up the recipe big time when we were little, Mom," they joke. Which shows you how much respect my culinary "prowess" wins in this address.

With *bagoong* and *tuyo* (salted fish), however, the alliances shift. In the interest of peace and cholesterol levels, I try to limit quite severely our intake of these two assault weapons in my cupboard, not because I am ceding the territory but because whenever I cook them, I have to deal with the unsavory task of scrubbing the stove and the kitchen walls to get the odor out. My *Pinoy*-ness, after all, has its limits. I hate the rancid smell of old oil, garlic, onions and whatever else that pervades a *Pinoy* kitchen and clings to one's clothes as tenaciously as body odor.

But sometimes, just sometimes, nothing hits the spot better than *bagoong* and/or *tuyo*. One of Carlo's favorite dishes is *binagoongan* (pork cooked in shrimp paste) and I cook it whenever I feel like being a good mother. And then there's the Mexican mango that we grudgingly eat, as long as they are the right ripeness and are on sale. I mean, if you're a Cebuano in America, how can you eat this red-green and round, uhm—thing—without washing it down with the exotic saltiness of *bagoong*?

No matter how much I try, however, I cannot make Maia empathize with our need for *bagoong* and *tuyo*. For her, they are merely weird and stinky; for Carlo, Jaja and I, they are remembrances of past pleasures.

Eating *bagoong* brings me back to my adolescent years at UP High, when at recess, I would watch with fascination the way the ambulant vendor would expertly peel and slice *manggang hilaw* (green mango) and slather it with the pink, salty substance before wrapping it in an old test paper picked up from god-knows-which dump in the campus. The taste was only a part of the pleasure, the rest came from the sinning. Forbidden from eating such unsanitary food, we naturally did so with gusto. More importantly, the vendor positioned herself at the far side of our building, where we could see our crushes playing ball in the adjacent field.

My association with *bagoong* goes way back, when I was little and my *yaya* boiled *kamoteng kahoy* (cassava) dug from our backyard and dipped it in *ginamos* (the Cebuano version) before feeding it to me. I loved sinking my teeth in the chewy root crop and feeling the salty liquid run down my chin before catching it with my finger, which I would then lick. I also cherished my *yaya's* stories of witches and *encantos* (spirits) that usually accompanied this ritual.

Tuyo, which is more a Tagalog delicacy, does not trigger as much nostalgia as *buwad danggit* (the dried fish of Cebu) but because it is more available in America than the Cebuano version, I have to live with it. It's no big deal because it goes well with the *champorado* (chocolate rice) that Jaja often craves for on weekends when we can indulge our quirks. Whenever someone from the Philippines comes to visit, however, my sister knows that *buwad* is right up there in my wish list, well ahead of *rosquillos, otap*, and the *hopiang munggo* from Kim Chung Tin in Echague.

I know, I know. Too much salt is bad. Too much fat clogs the arteries. Like most people my age, I bow to the dogma of low-fat and healthy—most of the time. But can anyone completely denounce the food that once defined one's days? I can't—maybe because my taste buds are directly linked to my emotions. And sometimes, for an expat like me, it is as much a matter of survival as it is of preference.

•*Filipinas* Magazine, September 1998•

115

Remembering Cebu
in California

PERUSING THE shelves of the Asian store in our neighborhood one afternoon, I did a double-take when I heard two women having a lively conversation. Overhearing a loud conversation among Filipinos is hardly unusual in this area, where the biggest concentration of Filipino expatriates live. In certain cities, in fact, notably Daly City, one can sometimes be lulled into thinking that she is in Manila, not California, because the native tongue is spoken everywhere.

But this was different; the women were speaking in Cebuano and, since I only know a few Cebuanos in the Bay Area, hearing someone actually speaking it in public was almost too good to be true. I hurriedly went and introduced myself as another Cebuano, thus initiating a long, boisterous exchange that involved tracing our family histories, establishing our hometowns, trying to determine who we knew from each other's clans and a lot of other topics that could easily perplex anyone who knew neither the language nor the kinship that pervaded Filipino culture.

Nahinangop, we said of ourselves. There is no direct translation for this word in English. It connotes eagerness and longing. It implies an absence and subsequently, a sense of fulfillment. Linguists may question this awkward attempt to translate what is basically a feeling, but I liken it to the thrill and enthusiasm one feels upon returning to the warm embrace of family after being stranded alone on an island.

I don't know if this is true of those who speak other Filipino languages but I've noticed that whenever Cebuanos meet casually, they don't use any other language to converse with except Cebuano. Celeste, my high school classmate and I, for example, may be speaking Tagalog or English in a gathering of friends, but when we address each other, we switch to Cebuano, complete with the proper intonation and the Cebuano way of pronouncing certain non-Cebuano words.

It just came naturally, this switch; we were not even conscious of it until someone pointed it out. And we could not explain why we did it except that it felt *hilas* (grossly pretentious) to do otherwise.

I find it strange and amusing how, now that I live in America, I sometimes get a strong longing for anything Cebuano. I've always considered myself *taga-Maynila*, or more specifically, a native of Quezon City where I've lived since I was three. I learned to speak Cebuano because my parents never learned how to speak Tagalog, so Cebuano became for me a language for the home, which I would immediately discard the moment I stepped out the door.

I'm sure, growing up, there was some embarrassment involved in speaking Cebuano because I remember being very proud that I spoke Tagalog like a native even if I always did poorly in my Pilipino classes. There is a big difference, after all, between reading and writing in a language and actually speaking it, and my language brain cells, straddling two tongues, never quite grasped the grammar of both.

As a young girl, my knowledge of anything Cebuano was hardly anything to boast about. Those days, we didn't travel much, not even within the country, except when it was absolutely necessary. The Manila-Cebu route was serviced mostly by slow, overcrowded ships that took almost three days to reach their destinations. Propeller planes took more than two bumpy hours (compared to the present-day forty-five minutes by jet). Needless to say, it took my parents a lot of years after we moved from Cebu to Quezon City to return to the old hometown for a vacation.

My connection to my Cebuano roots therefore was, at best, flimsy and occasional. I got a huge dose of it when relatives came to visit. Since we were the only family on both sides who were actually Manila-based, everyone who had business in Manila stayed with us. There was never a time during my younger years when we did not have cousins who came to study in Manila (sometimes as many as five) living with us. And when graduation time came, my aunts and uncles descended upon us, bringing with them the delicacies, the fruits, and the spices that were uniquely Cebuano, regaling me with stories about *enkanto* and *wakwak* (supernatural beings) while satiating my senses with the taste and aroma of home-cooked Cebuano dishes.

To this day I still wake up in the middle of the night aching for the taste of *torta, inasal, pirdis, humba, mahareal, tagaktak, puso* (pronounced differently from the Tagalog term for heart*), ginamos, buwad, Mandaue bibingka, budbud-kabog, bu-ongon, Carcar ampao, sisi, suriso, puto maya, tinughong* and other delicacies that populate my Cebuano memories. I am constantly in search of recipes for them, even if I know I can never hope to recapture the distinctive tastes that are permanently imprinted in my mind and my palate.

On my last visit to the province a few years ago, I felt a bit sad that the city that I knew as smaller and gentler than Metro Manila had transformed into a bustling metropolis, with the usual blight that accompanies such progress. The quiet street in Lahug where my parents' house used to be is now a jeepney route. Magellan Hotel is gone, replaced by the Ayala Mall. The old trees that used to shade Gorordo Avenue and Mango Avenue have been uprooted to give way to commercial buildings. However, despite all these signs of "progress," there was an energy and a comfort there that I did not feel in Metro Manila.

It is as if Cebuanos, with their legendary stubbornness, have collectively determined that despite the high-rises, the malls, and the urban traffic, they will remain what they always have been: small-town residents who know each other and care about each other's business.

While some people may deride the latter as nosiness, I choose to look at it through rose-tinted glasses and call it being home.

•*Filipinas* Magazine, November 2002•

Savoring Sagada

IF YOU STILL don't have a copy of Luis H. Francia's collection of travel essays cum memoir, *Eye of the Fish: A Personal Archipelago*, I strongly suggest you get yourself one, pronto. I bought my copy online a few weeks ago, and have been reading an essay each day. The slow reading pace is intentional: I want to savor the sights, sounds, and flavor of each place that he describes. Since Luigi and I move in different social circles, and he is seeing the Philippines from a Manhattanite's eyes, I am fascinated by his take on things. And I'm sure those of you who have traveled through our homeland, or who plan to do so, or even those who choose to be armchair travelers, will be just as drawn to Luigi's personal odyssey which took him from the Ilocos region all the way to Sulu. If only the book had a table of contents . . . but I'm nitpicking. It is a wonderful read.

My twenty-one-year-old daughter, Jaja, who has just come back from her own five-month backpacking journey (Australia, the Philippines, Bali, and London) doesn't want to read Luigi's book yet. She plans to write about her adventures and doesn't want her thoughts and impressions influenced by other folks who see the places she's been to with different eyes. I am listening to her stories, noting the lilt in her voice as she describes even the bad parts of her generally good experience and I am amazed, but not really surprised, at her joy. The excitement of flight, as I very well know, is transformative. Once you've tasted it, you're never quite the same again.

In the early '80s, shortly before all hell broke loose in our country, I went to Sagada with a group of friends. Sagada, a quaint town tucked away in the crannies of the Cordilleras, is a destination that is often mentioned by travelers to the Philippines as a must-see, and is part of the world map of backpackers who travel the Morocco-India-Nepal route. Many stories have been written about the burial caves that straddle its hillsides where the skeletons of the ancestors of the Kankanai are preserved.

When we went, we were not as interested in those gravesites as we were eager to soak in the legendary appeal of Sagada. For that was what we heard from regular visitors, that you don't just go to Sagada, you experience it. True enough, today I don't remember much of what we saw of the town but I can never forget the feeling of peace and serenity that the town allowed us. Sagada stilled the demons in my mind, however short our visit was.

We stayed with the artist Aster Tecson and his family. The house they were renting was about two kilometers away from the center of town and it was made entirely of wood that made strange noises when the frosty mountain wind blew through the wallboards. We loved that house. We had to sleep close to each other to keep warm and coordinate our trips to the outhouse. But somehow these "inconveniences" became part of the romance of Sagada and we never for a moment wished it were otherwise.

Beth, Aster's wife, had a constant supply of local tea—the best I've ever tasted, grown by the folks in another barrio, she said, and she led us to the edge of the precipice across the road from where we, city folk scared of heights, held on to each other as we peered at the huts and the tea fields below us.

Dinner was always early and by candlelight since Sagada at that time had no electric power. Then we would walk to town, briskly, to beat the oncoming dusk and the swiftly descending fog. Each night we would hang out in a coffee shop cum folk house run by this woman who was given to easy, vibrant laughter. Somehow, the beer that was the same brand as what we drank in Manila, tasted different in Sagada. It freed our mind and made us open up to each other, allowing our friendships to be sealed by sharing our deepest soul secrets. It was there in that coffee house

(Sagada coffee, by the way, is excellent), while we were singing our hearts out with other guests who became our instant friends, that the only guy in our group fell head over heels in love with one of the women with us. Sagada, we were warned, does that to people.

On our last night, we walked the long trek home, our path lighted only by the moon and the stars. We savored each breath that we took knowing that we were about to leave the pure Sagada air. We decided not to sleep and instead went up a hill, where there was a cottage beneath the pines and in the garden was a large tomb where the previous owner of the property was buried. From there, we watched the Sagada sunrise which was more glorious than anywhere else because it had for its backdrop the pure blue of the smog-free sky.

When we returned to Manila, I discovered that all the pictures I took of the place were ruined. Somehow I didn't despair because what I brought home from that trip was the Sagada in my mind. It was enough.

•*Filipinas* Magazine, September 2001•

Summers of Love

IT'S SUMMER and we, *Pinoy* expats, are in our element. The sun that used to darken our skins and drench our bodies with sweat is the same sun that now draws us out into the open. Unlike back home where we would hide behind umbrellas and cool shades, in our adopted country, we welcome the sun with bottles of sunblock. Forget the loneliness of winter; summer for us, tropical creatures, is the season of new possibilities.

And beautiful memories. Mangoes, iced *buko*, *siniguelas*, *atis*, beaches, swimming in streams, mosquitoes at night—remember?

Lately, I have been longing for my childhood summers at the University of the Philippines (UP) campus in Diliman and in Cebu, my home province. Perhaps it is the heat, or maybe I am at an age when details of my past are easier to remember than what I was saying just a moment ago.

My best memories are of those summers when my aunts, who lived in Carcar, Cebu, would arrive on campus to attend my cousins' graduations. They would come loaded with goodies—*ampaw, mamon, bu-ongon* (pomelo), multicolored shredded coconut balls and the many delicious pastries that the town was famous for. Wrapped in newspapers were large cuts of *inasal*, the Cebuano lechon that, unlike the Tagalog version, was stuffed with so much herb seasoning, it was delicious even without any sauce.

Those summers were better than Christmas. My aunts did not only bring us the good stuff, they would also cook their hearts out. Our suddenly busy kitchen would, for days, exude the aroma of lard, garlic, and the multi-faceted scents of the super-tasty dishes that were garnished with the luscious tales of small-town scandals that my notoriously talkative aunts would dish out.

I would watch them make *torta,* the Cebuano version of pound cake. Because I was the family's *torta* fanatic, my aunts said I had to learn how to bake one myself, but I never did. All I remember now is that a recipe of the genuine *torta* of my childhood, whose taste gave me so much unabashed pleasure, called for several dozen eggs and about a gallon of fresh lard that my aunts extracted from slabs of pork fat by frying them until they shrunk into crunchy chicharon.

When I grew older, we would go home to Cebu to attend the May fiesta in my father's hometown, Pinamungajan, a sleepy seaside town on the western side of the island. Just like many provincial towns, Pinamungajan would spring to life only once each year, when the townsfolk would open their doors to relatives coming home to enjoy the two-day feast. There the pleasures were different.

My father's clan is immense; at last count, there are at least 400 of us. Keeping track of all the relatives is almost impossible.

When the *bayle* (dance) took place at the town plaza, my male cousins would put on their best *banlon* shirts, slather their hair thick with Brilliantine and arm themselves with gin, *tuba,* and beer, to work up the courage to boogie to Elvis and twist to Chubby Checker. They would dance with me those rowdy numbers as a matter of filial responsibility since I was my father's child and somewhat of an oddity since I was "*taga-Manila*" (from the big city).

As soon as the slow music played, however, they would rush to the girls they were eyeing, eager for an excuse to hold them close. Their pleasure, however, never lasted. The next morning, most of them would be grumbling because the girls they thought they could romance turned out to be a relative.

The major personalities in my summer memories are long gone. True to their characters, my Carcar aunts passed away in style. One planned her funeral to the minutest detail, writing down her instructions in a notebook that had become worn out by the time she finally died. The other, not to be outdone, bought her funeral *saya* years before she actually passed away, and to make sure she would look her best when she laid in state, she would occasionally try on the gown and order alterations as she saw fit.

Many of my Pinamuganjan relatives are gone too, including my first cousin, an ex-soldier, who was incarcerated in Muntinlupa's Death Row for twenty years for allegedly ambushing the town mayor, but who eventually went back home a free man. Four months later, he died of a heart attack.

I have been telling Maia, my nine-year-old daughter, these stories of my childhood in the hope that she, whose summers revolve around swimming, ice-skating, and trips to Great America, will someday appreciate the food that shaped my taste buds and the relatives who helped define my character.

"Did your favorite cake taste as good as chocolate fudge cake, Mama?" she asks. "Did your cousins know how to ice-skate?"

There is a thirty-year and ten thousand-mile chasm between her concept of happiness and mine. But no matter. Like many expat parents, I cling to the hope that my U.S.-raised child will one day love the same things I love, even if all she can hold on to now are my stories.

It is summer, after all, a time for reverie, when I put aside, even only momentarily, the bittersweet reality that I have chosen a different world for my children.

•*Filipinas* Magazine, June 1997•

Terms of Endearment

NINE YEARS ago, my eighty-two-year old mother died. So quietly that my father, who was asleep beside her, did not notice that she had slipped away. It was a very peaceful death, my brother said, during the phone call that everyone with family far away dreads. Knowing that, however, was no consolation to me. I was then only a few weeks into my job, five months after I uprooted my three children to move to the San Francisco Bay Area in a quest for a new life.

"Come home," my brother said, "even if only for a few days." "But I don't have money," I sobbed. "And I will have to take Maia with me. Besides I am not entitled to vacation yet." Everything worked out, however, and I (with the still-nursing Maia) was able to say a proper final good-bye to my mother, who I hardly knew in the profound sense, having decided during my adolescence that she and my father were tyrants, out to make my life miserable.

The last time I talked to her was on her birthday, a few days before my children and I left for the States. She was already very frail then but her voice over the long-distance phone line was robust. "Take good care of the children," she said. "And don't forget to pray always." When I greeted her a happy birthday, she whispered, "It's taking so long ..." I didn't realize then what she meant, did not appreciate the one brief moment that she opened up to me.

I left the country without telling my parents that my marriage had ended and that I had sold all my material possessions so I could have a few hundred dollars to bring for my new life in California. I had my sister break the news to them, which she was only able to do much later. Characteristically, my father was shocked and angry, and wanted me to go home. My mother, however, was adamant. "Let her stay [in America] so she and the kids can start a new life. I have no doubt that she will thrive." Three days after her declaration of faith in me, she died.

For months afterwards, I would drive home from work each evening feeling her presence with me in the car. I would turn to look at the back seat to check if I could actually see her, but it was always empty. I would get this feeling of reassurance that she was watching over me, and we were finally able to connect as mother and daughter.

Memories of my mother and my regrets sweep over me whenever May comes along and the god of consumerism once again lures people into celebrating what I personally despise as an inane holiday: Mothers' Day.

As a mother, I am always tempted to tell my kids, "You know what I really want for this day, I want a break from being a mother. So go away." I never manage to articulate such dourness, however, because they serve me breakfast in bed and have flowers delivered. Whereupon I always feel so guilty, I forget about my exhaustion and my need for space.

Don't get me wrong. I love my kids, I live for them. All the major decisions I've made have been for their well-being. But having been a single parent for ten years (equivalent to twenty years of co-parenting, don't you think?), seeing them through the aches and pains of adolescence, through their anger at the world and at me, teaching them how to drive, keeping them schooled and clothed and fed on one income, waiting for them to come home late at night, watching them make mistakes, keeping my fingers crossed that I have taught them enough sense not to get killed, sick, take drugs or get pregnant (or not to get any girl pregnant)—whew, I need time to rest.

I have no need for the fuzzy-wuzzy once-a-year togetherness imposed by corny Mother's Day cards. We live like that everyday whenever the kids come home before I'm asleep, or when we are all in a good mood and have time to hang out before they rush out to be with their friends.

Okay, maybe my distaste for Mother's Day will wane when the kids are gone and living their own lives. By then, I'll probably be craving the rare occasions when they come home to me and we do things together again. Perhaps I will have a house by the beach in some other country, living the life I have been longing for, reading and listening to my music without interruption, writing my books. Perhaps I may even surprise them by cooking a feast.

But at this point, when I am still struggling with the challenges of motherhood, spare me the saccharine artificiality of Mother's Day.

•*Filipinas* Magazine, May 1998•

middle-age spread

Let's Get Physical

FINALLY, after a lifetime of denial and excuses, when my litany of justifications for remaining sedentary had turned awfully lame, I bit the proverbial bullet and signed up at a gym.

There were a host of reasons for my decision, foremost of which was—and I grit my teeth when I say this—my having turned fifty. Fifty! Which means I have already lived most of my life. And most likely, in twenty years (if I'm lucky to live that long), I will be bent, weak, and unable to enjoy the things that I enjoy now. Fifty! Suddenly, the words "menopause" and "osteoporosis" and "arthritis"—mere abstractions in my forties—have become real.

Then there were my pictures taken during our high school reunion earlier this year. In them, my happiness showed just as starkly as my fat biceps and my double chin. And my laughter at reading Anne Lamott's description of herself in a bathing suit—some of her body parts were still moving even when she had come to a complete halt (or something to that effect)—was tinged with pain. She could have been talking about me!

So I did it. It helped that a friend of mine also had his own compelling reasons to get in shape; misery shared made it tolerable. The process of signing up was the easy part. Starting my fitness program took another week of groaning and postponing until it became a self-respect issue. Then I actually had to go.

My trainer walked me through the machines and the weights; constantly soothing me with encouraging words ("you can do this easy") even as I looked with horror at the grotesque sights in the gym. People of all shapes and sizes, in costumes that made me blush in shame. Groaning, panting, faces contorting, sweating—if you close your eyes for a moment, you would think you're in a Marquis de Sade movie. Tell me again, why am I here?

But then there would walk in front of me gorgeous justifications for the worthiness of exercise—taut muscles, flat stomachs, a posture that claimed the world as their playground—and my resolve would strengthen. If I couldn't realistically aspire to be like one of those well-shaped people, could I at least hope to catch their eye?

First stop, the bike for warm-up and to get my heart rate going. "Don't try to go too fast right away," my trainer cautioned. So I pushed the pedals at a "comfortable pace" which didn't turn out to be too comfortable after the first minute. My legs and my stomach started hurting, and I had to catch my breath. Do I really have to do this, I kept asking myself. Finally, I had to give up—my heart was pounding too furiously—and I clambered off the bike. The whole exercise took 5 minutes. Did I tell you what shape I was in?

Then came the leg curl, the leg extension, the double leg press, the lateral pull-down, the free weights, the overhead press, the back extension, the biceps and triceps machines, the abdominal curl. I watched the gym veterans do the routine and hey, I can do that easy, I told my trainer. I sat down on seats adjusted to my height, and started counting. One ... nothing happened, the machines wouldn't budge! Are you sure this one is not broken, I asked at one point. The trainer looked at me with an I've-seen-the-likes-of-you-so-many-times-before look before helping out. Eventually I was able to make some progress—one, two, three ... at about seven, my arms or legs (whichever was on the line) felt like they were going through an amputation and my mind was once again questioning the wisdom of such self-inflicted torture.

At the treadmill, I would will myself into daydreaming positive images, in an effort to lessen the agony of the walk. As I huffed and puffed my way toward my goal, I would imagine myself in a bathing suit, with no misplaced bulges. But such visions didn't last because my overactive mind would swing to food, heaping platefuls of *adobo, lechon, kare-kare, biko,* the pork barbecue that my sister's neighbor in Quezon City sold every afternoon at his street-corner stall. Other times it would be sushi and chicken teriyaki, then crème brulee and tiramisu. That must be what dying was all about, an entire menu of the most fat-laden dishes flashing before your eyes, taunting you with their aromas, overpowering even the smell of sweat that enveloped you.

After getting used to my gym routine and, in the process, gaining a much-improved sense of self-respect, I could finally say I was hooked. I was functioning better. No more sleeping aids for me. A twenty-minute walk was now a piece of cake. Forty-five minutes of cardiovascular workout? How about an hour?

My daydreaming while doing the treadmill had even assumed a new dimension. I am trekking mountains and running trails. Waltzing in Vienna in a figure-hugging gown and rockin' in London. Sometimes I'm in Paris or Florence sitting in a restaurant with food, glorious food, at my bidding. Yes, I have conquered my physical laziness and I am unabashedly proud of myself.

Now if I could only stick to a healthy diet.... did I mention cake?

•*Filipinas* Magazine, October 1999•

The Golden Rules

IT'S THE MORNING after People Power II, and our homeland is now led by a woman who, at fifty-something, starts a new career as president. Cory Aquino was about that age when she assumed the same office. Women in our age group should take heed: To be fifty and healthy is to have an entire future before us, a future that will allow us to reinvent ourselves based on the wisdom we have accumulated through the years, a future that we can define any way we like because we have raised our families, paid our dues, discovered our true substance, and outgrown the expectations imposed on us by society. Life from hereon can only be one big party.

Being in our fifties today is not like it was in our parents' time. The Baby Boomer generation—that mighty pack of spoiled brats to which we belong and which has never stopped trying to change the world according to its terms—has transformed the concept of aging so radically that we now have more freedom and more options to live, look, and think younger.

Yet, we cannot deny our body clocks. "When I turned fifty, it seemed like my body parts started malfunctioning," someone once remarked. We are now in menopausal mode and our hormones are so out of whack that our families sometimes wonder if we are the same woman they used to know. It's embarrassing and maddening to be having hot flashes in inopportune moments and losing our temper for the most trivial reasons. Worse, we sometimes wake up with aching joints, clogged ears, and an inability to remember what we did yesterday.

Some friends and I were laughing hysterically at the foibles of being "golden-agers" when we realized that we still have decades ahead of us and we should make sure that they are fun, productive, and fulfilling. So we came up with this list of reminders that we think women our age should keep in mind:

1. **Stay healthy.** If you have to go to the bathroom every five minutes or get sick at the first whiff of temperature change, it can put a damper on your plan to conquer the world. So keep those muscles moving and your heart pumping. You need not turn athletic but you should at least follow a regimen that makes you feel good.

2. **Ignore the standard of beauty peddled by fashion magazines.** At fifty, you have earned the right to determine the body shape you are most comfortable in. Who cares if you have bulges in the wrong places? You have lived long enough to be interesting and substantive, unlike those reed-thin models who are still groping for happiness and self-knowledge. Been there, done that. Besides, there's nothing more pathetic than a fifty-year-old woman trying to look twenty.

3. **Flirt.** Not the kind you did in your youth or when you were going through your mid-life crisis in your forties, when the intention was to snare a man. This time you flirt because it's fun. All it takes is a little more time in front of the mirror, dressing better, looking people straight in the eye, trying to connect more deeply with the person you are having a conversation with. Flirting with your partner can trigger fireworks that can make both of you look and feel younger.

4. **Eat well.** Not just healthy, because often that means deprivation. Savor to the fullest the sensuality of eating good food—the sight, the smell, the texture, the effect it has on your

well-being. Eating is one of life's greatest pleasures and to deprive yourself of it when you don't have to because you're afraid to gain weight is foolish and masochistic. I'm not saying that you should be a glutton. At fifty, you already know your limits.

5. **Develop your mind.** There's nothing more aging than a mind that has stopped growing. Even if you've spent a good part of your life cooped up at home taking care of your family, it's never too late to catch up with the bigger world. Read. Surf the Net. Attend lectures. Travel. Pursue an interest. Take up a cause. Expand your horizons beyond the comfortable niche you have created for yourself and your family.

6. **Write.** You are a living repository of the wisdom of the ages. Don't you want to share it with your children and grandchildren so they will be spared the mistakes you've suffered and learned from? Forget about style and grammar (unless you are thinking of publication). Just write whatever comes to mind. Let the children figure it out later.

7. **Let go of your male dependence.** I'm not saying break up your relationship. But develop your sense of independence so that if you want to go somewhere to nurture your soul and your husband prefers to stay home, you can go by yourself. It's better than sulking and seething. At our age, we appreciate the need for silences and occasional separations.

8. **Avoid people and situations that make you uncomfortable.** You are no longer running for Miss Congeniality so you don't have to have everyone like you. Rude, obnoxious people can give you wrinkles. Those needy men who used to arouse your maternal instincts are major turn-offs. We've done our share of nurturing others; it's time to nurture ourselves.

9. **Develop friendships.** Get in touch with those you have neglected because of the demands of family life. Form new

ones with like-minded people. Schedule a regular get-together with girlfriends—you are each other's support group and therapist. Don't be afraid to develop deep friendships with men who are fun to talk to. They often offer a different perspective on things and are just as eager to have conversations with women of substance.

10. **Above all, appreciate yourself.** In a radio commercial, Lauren Hutton, the top model of the '60s, says, "I will never trade my fifty-year-old body for a twenty-year-old mind." That about sums up what we all should feel. Battle-scarred, menopausal, somewhat rotund, a little hard of hearing, short-term memory failing—so what? We are the women pioneers of the Boomer Generation and we will still change the world.

•*Filipinas* Magazine, March 2001•

Intimations of Mortality

HAVE YOU EVER had one of those insightful moments when it suddenly occurs to you—from out of nowhere—that your remaining years on earth are much less than what you have already used up? I woke up one morning with this disconcerting realization, around my birthday two years ago, and it has lodged in the periphery of my consciousness ever since.

The issue of mortality assumed center stage recently, when some very dear friends were stricken with serious ailments due presumably to a youth carelessly lived and/or the strong sense of denial of the inevitability of aging that is reportedly common among Baby Boomers.

Despite our daily ration of health-related warnings from the media, we are still reluctant to consider the possibility that we may no longer be able to do what we want to. When we hear disturbing news, we get scared for a few minutes and then we say, nah that can't happen to me, I feel younger than my actual age and I still have the energy to change the world. And then one day, the news hits home—someone we actually know has cancer, or had a stroke, or died unexpectedly because of some previously undetected illness. That's when we scramble to have our check-ups and resolve to make some long- overdue lifestyle changes.

We start an exercise program and try to cut down the fat, the sodium, and the calories from our diet. We stop drinking alcohol. But just when we think we have this illness thing licked, we hear of someone our age who is slim, athletic, and a long-time vegetarian, who has died from a stroke, and we pause from our frantic health binge and ask if our self-inflicted punishment is really worth it.

Can it be that our elders are correct, that when it's our time to go, no amount of healthy living will save us? And what if we don't die right away, and instead suffer years of helplessness? We ask each other these questions—comparing ailments is usually topic number one in any get-together—and come nowhere near getting a satisfactory answer. Meantime we hedge our bets by compromising between eating healthy and living *la vida loca*.

I tried going on a no-meat, low-fat, low-salt diet once. It was easy the first week but then I got a whiff of my neighbor's *adobo* and I started hankering for pork slathered with sweet-sour, garlicky sauce. The desire stayed with me, chipping away at my resolve until the thought of feasting on meat became almost an obsession. I would daydream of *mechado, lechon*, and the Cebuano dish *humba* (with lots of pork fat swimming in soy beans and soy sauce). When I woke up craving a McDonald's hamburger (which to me is the equivalent of groveling for food), I knew that I had reached my limit.

I reverted to my not-exactly-healthy diet but in moderation. I tell anyone who cares to listen that I eat whatever I want—but in smaller quantities—while I am still able because a few years from now, I may have to follow some dietary restrictions. And when that time comes, I expect to be able to accept such restrictions with grace because I've had my fill. Ah, the lies I weave just to justify my appetites.

Beyond watching our food intake, living healthy also means being happy. Of course, the concept of happiness is defined differently by each individual but, if we are to believe the gospel of self-help books, it means slowing down, doing what we want and getting rid of our stresses. Which means that happiness is beyond the reach of working stiffs who have no choice but to drive through horrible commute traffic each day to earn a paycheck that can hardly meet the bills. Like 90 percent of the workforce in this country.

A friend of mine seems to have mastered the art of this looking-at-the-glass-as-half-full-instead-of-half-empty approach to life. Since she can't control her two-hour daily commute, she considers it as "quiet time" where she can listen to soothing music without interruption from her kids. She spends part of her lunch hour walking and appreciating the wildflowers by the roadside, the scents in the air, the warmth of the noonday sun. These rituals have done her so much good, she says, that her blood pressure is now normal and she is able to handle the stresses of her life better. "You just have to grab whatever trickle of happiness comes your way," she tells me.

That perhaps is the key to living well. Instead of setting our standard of happiness so high that it's almost impossible to achieve (a prime example is winning the Lotto and living happily ever after), we can focus our attention on simple, attainable things. Like driving to the park at the end of a hectic day at work to watch the sunset. Or shutting out the rest of the world while perusing old books in a used bookstore. Or even just being completely present when the children start talking about their day (instead of responding with the perfunctory *uh-huh* while our minds are somewhere else).

The next time you wake up with an ache in your joints or discontent in your soul, pay attention. It could just be the pain of a life not yet fully lived.

•*Filipinas* Magazine, July 2001•

Second Chances

THERE WAS A story that made the rounds in Manila in the '70s, when martial law and the romance of revolution were at their peak, that a military officer in civilian clothes who was returning to his post in Isabela in a crowded bus, was handed a note that said, "*Mistah, pangalawang buhay mo na ito* (this is your second life)." *Mistah* is a term classmates at the Philippine Military Academy use to address each other. The note purportedly came from Vic Corpus, the renegade Army lieutenant who had joined the New People's Army (NPA) in Isabela.

Apocryphal, it turned out. Vic said it never happened although he had some close and more interesting encounters with his *mistahs* (who were specifically ordered to capture him) at various times during his Isabela days. What was not apocryphal was how Col. Gringo Honasan, then riding the height of his popularity shortly after the EDSA People Power Revolution in 1986, greeted for the first time his PMA upperclassman who was newly released from prison: "Sorry, sir, for taking fifteen years to do this."

What Gringo was referring to was the student strike at PMA he and a few of his classmates were clandestinely planning with Vic, who was then their instructor. Their goal was to expose corruption in the academy; D-day would have been January 1971. On December 30, 1970, however, Vic raided the PMA armory and defected to the NPA, thereby triggering intensified security in the academy and aborting the planned strike.

These memories came back to me not just because Vic and Gringo were again in the news in the Philippines (this time as adversaries) but also because they both illustrated the idea of *pangalawang buhay*, a second chance at life, a concept that had always fascinated the story-gatherer in me. In the same way, the amazing story of Marlene Macaranas-Manuel, who called her family on her fifty-fourth birthday from a hospital in Baghdad when she was already being mourned as dead from that bombing at the UN headquarters, had piqued my personal attention. Talk about the ultimate second chance!

Pangalawang buhay. I hear it said in various circumstances, such as when one finds happiness after a heartbreak, when one escapes a near-death experience or discovers a new passion amidst the detritus of a major failure, when one is presented another opportunity to make a historical difference or recovers from a serious illness. A second wind connotes expiation, resurrection, and optimism. It is even sweeter when it happens after one has hit rock bottom.

Yet second chances also suggest an obligation—to do right, to not waste time, to enjoy the magic of each moment because we may not have such chance again. And this is where we often stumble. How many occasions have we let pass because we did not recognize them as providential opportunities to "pick up the pieces"? How much regret can our hearts endure when we discover, on hindsight, that we could have done something but didn't?

When I had Maia, my youngest child, eight years after I had Jaja, I would jokingly tell my perplexed friends that I wanted the chance to correct the parenting mistakes I made with my two older kids. The reality, of course, was more complex. I wasn't just honing my parenting skills with Maia, she was also the impetus I needed to carve out a new life from the ruins of a failed marriage. Her birth and the unexpected opportunity to immigrate were second chances I was handed and I wasn't going to squander them.

I have noticed among people I know that the risk of passing up golden opportunities—out of inattention, smugness, or fear—goes up several notches as one grows older. Yet it is at this time in our lives that we are freer to change or edit our life scripts. The signs may be all around us, like we lose our long-time job and getting a new one of similar gravity is highly unlikely, our children are grown and our retirement funds are adequate, a cottage by the beach in our hometown is up for sale, and the lure of a more relaxed existence is getting stronger each passing day. Why would we insist on ignoring these cosmic cues when they may be snatched away at any time? There is no such thing as being too old to discover new frontiers, whether within ourselves or in the outside world. There is no statute of [age] limitations for taking another shot at life.

I am taking this issue of second chances to heart because I have realized that the comfortable lives we lead in America can easily lull us to inaction. True, there is something to be said for the stability of a predictable existence but if there is in you, as there is in many of us, a longing for a cause or a passion that makes you feel more alive, then perhaps it is time to reexamine your priorities and respond to that flame that has never died. Maybe the second chance that you need will not really alter your life as you know it. If you're one of the lucky ones, all you might have to do is brighten the colors of your personal canvas, not chuck it altogether.

To pass up a second chance is not only foolish, it's blasphemous. It is a gift not given to everyone, this privilege of having the universe realign itself to create possibilities out of dreams.

•*Filipinas* Magazine, October 2003•

The Rhythm of the Dance

It's Friday and almost midnight, the time of week when I should be giving my middle-aged body a rest. Somehow what used to be my end-of-the-week bliss—tucked in bed with a wonderful book—seems too tame, too boring now. There's the rest of the week after all to indulge in quiet, simple pleasures. But Friday night?

I still remember the first time Maia saw me all dressed up and ready to go. She looked at me with a what's-my-mother-up-to-now kind of look, a blend of incredulity and amusement. Almost like the look I gave her older siblings when I saw some of the friends they brought home. You know, that you-gotta-be-kidding look, which was a precursor to some lively conversations afterwards. My daughter has since become blasé about my weekly nocturnal activity, already a welcome ingredient in the landscape of our lives. I'm happy, and I get off her case, which, to a teenager like her, is enough reason to shove me out the door.

I'm talking about going ballroom dancing, the national craze that swept the Philippines for years. I am a "late-bloomer" in this arena, getting into it only this year when the hordes back home are starting to retire their dancing shoes and are already getting ready for the next craze to sweep them off their feet.

It was not for lack of desire that I took up ballroom dancing this late in the game. I have always loved dancing. As a little girl, I wanted to take up ballet but my father refused and sent me to piano lessons instead (as a result and to my regret, I never learned how to play). But that didn't stop me from dancing to "The Blue Danube" and daydreaming about wearing a tutu for long spells, whenever I was alone.

Growing up, I learned to boogie the way it was done during our time, by tying a piece of rope or cloth to a doorknob and holding on to it while figuring out the steps to Elvis's "Jailhouse Rock." It helped that I had natural rhythm and the ability (with a lot of patience and determination) to pick up techniques from regularly watching such TV shows as *Dance-O-Rama* and *Jam Session*. By the time the Beatles came along, I was quite an expert boogie dancer and I would have gotten really good if only the boys I danced with had the same perseverance to learn some style from TV shows.

It was an easy transition to Mashed Potato, the Boogaloo, the Jerk and Soul—the dances of our era that look so embarrassingly stupid now—although I gave up on Watusi and Elephant Walk in high school because Thelma, our class beauty and dancing queen, made all of us look like dorks when she danced those with a grace that we could only dream about. The Bye-bye, of course, was a no-brainer. We learned it quickly because it was simple and it allowed us to hold our partners while keeping our bodies apart, to pass the strict rules of our teacher who took it upon herself to temper our raging adolescent hormones.

With *Dancetime with Chito*, the ultimate dance program on TV that taught the more sophisticated Latin dances, I was able to pick up the cha-cha and bossa nova and some other steps I could no longer remember. I learned to recognize the beat and coordinate my feet with the sway of my body so I felt like I was really dancing (as opposed to just moving in time to the music). We know now that in exercise, beyond a certain point, the pain turns to pleasure. So it was with me with dancing. Though unschooled in the fine points, I was confident enough to dance to whatever music was played, and that made a lot of difference at the proms, jam sessions, and frat balls that were our standard entertainment fares then.

And then real life happened. As our generation started marrying and parenting, the dance parties dwindled. Those of us who remained single longer were able to occasionally manage a night out when the Circus band was the biggest rage on Roxas Blvd. But the dances and the rhythms of the 'seventies failed to distract many of us away from the deadly march of revolution. Worse, the guys I went out with—and the one I eventually married— were not into dancing (had I been wiser, it should have been a prerequisite).

So here I am thirty years later, trying to make up for lost time. *Balikbayan* visits to Manila whetted my appetite but it still took a while for me to get into ballroom dancing here because unlike back home, DIs (dance instructors) are not easy to come by in North America. The first step was to find a partner or a group of friends who are just as passionate about learning the proper dance patterns and finding the dance clubs we feel comfortable in.

But believe me, there is a lot to be said about ballroom dancing as a total experience. The coordinated swaying and swirling, the excitement of the beat, even the pleasure of dressing up are simply wonderful. There is nothing much like it in this age of high blood pressure and diminishing energy levels. So if you haven't yet picked up ballroom dancing, go give it a try. It's good for the heart, the soul, the body fat and those pesky arthritic knees. And it might just be the spark you need to make you fall in love all over again.

•*Filipinas* Magazine, November 2003•

politics is
personal

September Memories

I wake up early to the kind of morning songs are written for: bright sunshine, a slight breeze, birds chirping. Today, we are shooting some footage for the launching of ABS-CBN's nationwide simulcast and I, as scriptwriter, get to go up the tower with the cameraman. Pretty daring on my part, since I'm terrified of heights.

When I get to the station, I am greeted by the blood-curdling sight of Metrocom soldiers guarding the closed gates. My co-workers are gathered across the street, looking scared. "What happened?" I ask. Murmurs of "they've taken over" and the dreaded words: "martial law" and "arrests."

I rush home in a panic. Dodong, my brother, and Princess, my sister-in-law, both known leftists, were still asleep when I left. I see a strange car in a driveway, making my heart jump. Turns out Bobby, my college buddy, had heard the rumor (the airwaves are silent), and is there to help. Dodong tells me to disappear for a few days while we assess the situation, and then he is gone. Princess is rousing the kids—Fidel, 11; Leonid, 10; Lian, 7 — to take them to their grandma's house. Auring, our househelp, is already burning papers in the backyard and I grab armloads to help. But there's just too many of them and I have to leave too.

In my friend's house hours later, we remain clueless. No radio or TV broadcasts still. The rumors are chilling: many have been arrested including Ninoy Aquino; someone shot Enrile. Restless, I decide to check on our house. My friend offers to drive. As we turn into our street, I almost die. Military trucks are in our driveway. Soldiers in full battle gear surround the house, their armalites pointed at the windows. Others are loading books and documents in the trucks.

I slide down the car seat to avoid being seen and find myself looking up at the canopy of trees that line our street. The afternoon sun is still shining bright and the air is filled with the sweet aroma of jasmines and *kalachuchi*, but I—and the rest of the nation—have lost my innocence.

1984, September

I am meeting G, a woman from the Davao underground, in Makati so I put on makeup more carefully than usual and wear a white cotton dress. Years of dodging military operatives have taught me that the best disguise is to dress well. Since G and I are going to a big rally at the Quezon City Welcome rotunda, we decide to eat a sumptuous lunch at an upscale restaurant where no one suspects that he or she is in the company of someone "wanted" in Mindanao.

Reaching the rally site, I pin my press card on my white dress. The demonstration is in full swing but there is an air of dread because the police contingent is bigger than usual. Anticipating trouble, some women journalists and I go up to the top floor of the hospital that overlook the rotunda to get a better view.

The rally leaders are exhorting the crowd of thousands to disperse and regroup at the Santo Domingo Church a few blocks away to escape the police phalanx. Since Quezon Avenue is already blocked, the rallyists move toward the side streets. And then it happens. Military trucks loaded with soldiers start coming. The police are running after the demonstrators and we hear shots fired.

We walk briskly to Santo Domingo to join other journalists. The marchers who have reached the compound are in a frenzy, talking about a carnage. A woman rushes up to me and says, "Did you hear? Your nephew Fidel has been shot!" I actually feel my blood stop in its tracks, my knees turn to putty, and I keel over. My friend, Jun Factoran, catches me but everything becomes a blur, like a slow-motion film with an unfocused camera. Randy David and Marites Vitug get me into Randy's van which careens through the military barricades toward the hospital.

A nurse leads us to a room to meet the doctor who is heading the team of surgeons about to operate on Fidel. He has lost a lot of blood and has to be operated on immediately, we are told. We beg to see him but he is already sedated. "Don't worry," the doctor assures. "He will pull through." (Days later, when the crisis was over, he would admit he was not that optimistic at that point.)

The agony of waiting begins.

Hour one: A crowd gathers outside the restricted area where we are cloistered. Randy calls to break the bad news to Dodong, who is with Princess and Lian in Australia, teaching. Art, who was with Fidel when he was shot, brings me the blood-soaked t-shirt showing two bullet holes, one in front, the other in the back. Leonid arrives from his exams, very shaken. We are all too shocked to cry. Or even to comfort each other.

Hour two: A radio reporter summons me saying that my brother is on the phone. "Were they really shooting at the people?" he asks the moment he hears me. "Yes," I say. "Many are here now, wounded." It turns out we are on-the-air. He asks for Leonid. I use the other phone to call home and check on my kids.

Hour three: Food arrives from sympathizers but no one eats. I go out to the hallway to greet the people who are there. They will wait for news, they say, however long it takes. I am touched but am too numb to convey my deep appreciation. I nod like a zombie. Some reporters want to interview me but I refuse. Stop being such vultures, I want to scream. I am suddenly ashamed of my profession, at how we (and I am just as guilty as the others) prey on the misery of others to get our stories. How different the view is from the other side.

Hour four: Leonid has gone home to study for his exams. Alone in the waiting room, I cling to the doctor's assurance that Fidel will be all right, to avert my growing panic. Why is it taking so long?

Hour five: The doctor enters, visibly exhausted. "We're stabilizing him now," he says. The bullet had entered his back, missing his spine by a centimeter, shattering his liver, diaphragm and lung and exited his chest very close to his heart. I close my eyes tight and say a prayer for the thousandth time. He's alive!

Fidel is wheeled out after midnight, heavily bandaged and sedated. Try to wake him, the nurse instructs. I massage his arms and whisper in his ear over and over: "Fidel, you are going to get well." He moans. "Fidel," I say with conviction, "we are not going to let them defeat us!" He opens his eyes for a few seconds. Enough to whisper very weakly, "*P_____ nila.*" Yeeeeesss! I slump on the chair and finally weep in relief, my makeup and my tears staining my white dress.

• *Filipinas* Magazine, September 2000 •
Originally titled "September Notes"

Paradigm Shift

LIKE MOST Filipinos born a few years after World War II, I grew up under the shade of America the Mighty, America the Benevolent Protector, America the Friend for All Seasons. Everything "Made in the U.S.A."—from toys to shoes to comic books—were considered better; owning them meant one has bragging rights and veto privileges over anyone who dared ask to touch or borrow those cherished possessions.

In our early elementary years, we were even taught the U.S. National Anthem (which we thought started out as "Jose can you see") and "America the Beautiful," singing them in our classrooms like nursery rhymes. At that time, the flag ceremony that started our school week involved singing the Philippine National Anthem in English. "Land of the morning/ child of the son returning/with fervor burning ..." The Pledge of Allegiance too was recited in English and we, whose natural language was Tagalog, would let the words slide off our tongues without really understanding what they meant, in much the same way we recited the Lord's Prayer and the Hail Mary, where we merely memorized the sounds, not the words.

When then-President Diosdado Macapagal (father of the current Philippine president) changed the celebration of Philippine Independence from July 4 to June 12, in 1962, we were baffled. June 12, 1898, the day General Emilio Aguinaldo declared the country's independence from Spain, was just too incomprehensible for us who were reared on the belief that it was the U.S. that granted us independence after the Second World War, on July 4, 1946.

Unknown to most of us then, Aguinaldo and the veterans of the Philippine Revolution had always celebrated June 12 as Independence Day, even after they surrendered to the Americans. The annual ceremony would take place in Kawit, Cavite where Ambrosio Rianzares Bautista, from the balcony of Aguinaldo's house, publicly read the actual Proclamation of Independence in 1898. In 1940, they moved the celebration to the Luneta, with then President Manuel Quezon as guest of honor. Quezon reportedly agreed to declare June 12 as an official holiday but the war started before he could do so.

It was not until 1960 that the National Historical Association formally petitioned the President and Congress to adopt June 12 as Philippine Independence Day. The petition was a result of the effort of Gabriel Fabella, a retired history professor of the University of the Philippines, who researched historical documents and determined that July 4 was not a date chosen by the Filipinos but by the U.S. Congress. Fabella pointed out that the celebration of the country's independence should be on the day it was declared by its people, not on the day it was recognized by a foreign power.

When the switch to June 12 happened in 1962, Aguinaldo was still able to attend the festivities as the guest of honor. Despite grumbling from certain quarters about the appropriateness of the date, that year's Independence Day celebration reportedly drew a crowd of "at least one million people," according to Macapagal, "whereas in previous celebrations on July 4, only from two to three thousand came."

[According to the book, *100 Events That Shaped the Philippines*, Macapagal later wrote that the change of date was also a result of the rejection by the U.S. House of Representatives of a $73 million additional war payment bill on May 9, 1962 which "caused indignation among the Filipinos".]

Looking back, the date change was a propitious event because it triggered the slow weaning of the Philippines from the giant shadow of the United States. For one thing, we started singing the National Anthem in Pilipino, a ritual that has now been so ingrained in us that to this day, despite hearing it only very occasionally here in America, most of us can still sing it by heart. (In contrast, many of us have not really memorized the "Star Spangled Banner.")

The emergence of June 12, 1898 as a day of commemoration also encouraged among Filipinos a consciousness of the significance of the Philippine Revolution against Spain, a logical source of pride for a country so used to being colonized. It must have been around this time that the pro-American history books that had been standard fare in our schools were replaced by more nationalistic ones. Subsequently, as more historical accounts about the ugly side of the American occupation of the Philippines emerged, the image of the United States as savior and benefactor began to crumble.

By the late 1960s, when the Filipino youth learned to stage massive demonstrations against government and "American imperialism," the nation was already in the throes of a love-hate relationship with the United States. There was anger for sure, against the social and political costs of the U.S. bases, against the continuing subservience of Filipino politicians to U.S. demands, against the ingrained colonial mentality that had stymied the emergence of a truly Filipino national consciousness. Added to this was the unstinting support of the U.S. government for the Marcos government, which was then already becoming increasingly unpopular.

Ironically, it was in the 1960s and the early 1970s that the "brain drain" happened, bringing to America the biggest number of professional Filipinos as immigrants. And, like it or not, American culture will always be a significant factor in our consciousness.

This month as we celebrate the 105th anniversary of our homeland's triumph against Spain, let us also reflect on the other superpower that imposed its will on us on December 10, 1898, under the legal cover of the Treaty of Paris. It was glossed over by the biased history books of our youth, but now we know that the Philippine-American War that ensued was fierce and brutal, and it displayed in full measure the Filipinos' capacity for heroism in defense of the country's sovereignty.

Would that we will always be so proud.

• *Filipinas* Magazine, June 2003 •

A Heroic August

IT WAS ONE of those languid, tropical Sunday afternoons common in the Augusts of our lives back home. I was alone in the house so I dug up some of my "milestone objects," bits of memories that I kept to mark significant events in my life. I had the radio tuned to an "oldies" station, partly because I was in that kind of mood, and partly because I was not interested in listening to the frenzied reporting that radio journalists always did when a celebrity returned home.

The memory of that day—August 21, 1983—will forever be etched in my consciousness, as it is in the consciousness of countless Filipinos. It was our November 23, 1963 (the day JFK was shot) and our September 11, 2001—a tragedy so shocking and senseless, it would redefine our perceptions like nothing else before then.

It was around 1:00 p.m. when I started paying attention to the radio broadcast; the music was interrupted by up-to-the-minute on-the-spot reporting by radio journalists who were trying to outdo each other in announcing what they did not really know. I heard them say, "Ninoy Aquino was led off the plane. Shots were heard." I felt my blood freeze. No, this could not be happening, I thought. I stopped what I was doing and ran to the TV. Nothing there. Increasing panic on the radio: where was he? No one saw him leave the airport and the throngs of welcomers were becoming increasingly agitated.

Everything became a blur. I remember being on the phone non-stop, with my journalist-friends, with my family, trying to reach my husband to tell him to come right home, the radio and TV blaring, my heart feeling squeezed by the thunderbolt of emotions that swept through me, my eyes smarting from tears of anger and frustration.

At the airport VIP lounge, Ninoy's mother, sisters and brothers were waiting, hoping to be allowed into the jetway so they could see Ninoy emerge from the plane. Everyone was nervous; there were already speculations that he would be whisked directly to a prison cell. The local-based foreign correspondents were milling around the jetway, not being allowed in but close enough to hear the plane door open, then the shots and the commotion.

As Lupita Kashiwahara, Ninoy's sister, recalls, when the correspondents started running out, she immediately rushed to her husband, Ken, then an ABC News correspondent, who was with Ninoy on the plane. He was very shaken, and could only mutter "The bastards shot him, they shot him." Lupita wanted to know if Ninoy was dead but Ken could not bring himself to utter the word.

Outside the airport, the crowd of about fifteen thousand well-wishers was becoming increasingly restless under the sweltering August sun. At one point, a cheer erupted when they thought they saw Ninoy emerge. For a split second, Lupita thought—wished—the dire news was wrong, that Ninoy was actually alive, but it was Butz, their younger brother, who the crowd mistook for Ninoy.

Later that day, as the mourning and the anger spread like a conflagration across the nation, the Aquino family rushed to the Fort Bonifacio hospital where they were told Ninoy was. Lupita remembers that when she got a call from a military officer, she screamed, "*Buhay o patay?*" (Is he alive or is he dead?), but the voice at the other end just said to go to the hospital.

After being given the bureaucratic run-around, the family was finally able to go up to the second floor. It was then that Lupita, who had stayed behind to sign the logbook, heard her two sisters scream a primal scream and she knew then without a doubt that Ninoy was dead. His body was in a gurney, the blood on his clothes still fresh. "There was a slight smile on Ninoy's face," Lupita said, "and I found solace in the knowledge that he was at peace."

One of the most enduring images of that day was Ninoy's mother, Doña Aurora Aquino, caressing her son's face, his clothes smeared in martyr's blood. It was his mother, who remained stoic and prayerful all through those agonizing moments, who insisted that nobody touch her son's body. "Let the people see what they have done to him," she declared.

It was that heart-tugging image that reportedly got the people in power so agitated that they ordered the mainstream press to kill it. But it was too late; the proverbial genie was out of the bottle. As the throngs gathered at Ninoy and Cory's Times St. residence to pay tribute, the bell started ringing the countdown for the demise of the Marcos administration.

Where were you when Ninoy Aquino was assassinated? So many dreams have been sucked out of our idealism since then, so many frustrations have engulfed us. But this month, on the 20th anniversary of his martyrdom, let us pause and remember the supreme irony that one of our homeland's biggest tragedies led to our people's most glorious achievement in 1986. Out of the Marcos government's arrogance of power emanated its most monumental mistake.

Let us celebrate then that relatively brief moment in our history when we were united in grief and later in glory. We may never trek that road again. After all, there is, and should only be, one Ninoy Aquino.

• *Filipinas* Magazine, August 2003 •

Pain and Remembrance

FOR THOSE WHO write to live, there's nothing more rewarding—and humbling—than receiving responses from friends and total strangers who feel strongly enough about one's writing that they actually take the time to write a letter. My last two columns—on Jose Corazon de Jesus and on our "cyberbarangay"—have allowed me to connect with readers of various persuasions, some of whom even want to convert me or recruit me. And I have also heard from long-lost friends, who remember me as a "cute," "bubbly" and "mini-skirted" teenager who hung out with them in places long-since gone. (Dare I say anything about how I look now?)

One of them is Vic, a former activist and now a devout Christian, who had completely lost contact with our circle of friends and who wrote me a long, touching e-mail to refresh my memory of him and to ask about the others. His letter brought a wave of nostalgia, for those days in the early '70s in Manila which writer Pete Lacaba had immortalized as "days of disquiet, nights of rage." Then, we were passionate about our politics and our relationships, and we had this overwhelming desire to change the world.

Vic, more than I, was right there where the action was and he lent what I remember was his considerable singing talent to rallies, teach-ins and street theater presentations. One night, he reminded me, I was with his group when they "invaded" Butterfly restaurant—that folk-singing joint on the outskirts of the UP Diliman campus—where they sang revolutionary songs to the delight of the crowd.

Vic's letter also brought back a host of painful memories because not long after those heady days, martial law was declared and the group that was brought together by politics had to disperse.

This was what happened to some of our friends, Vic, and I share this story not just with you but with all who lived through that period in our country's history.

Shortly after my brother Dodong and his wife Princess were detained in Camp Crame in 1973, I got a late-night call from them. Since Dodong was in solitary confinement and not allowed phone calls, I knew right away that it was bad news. His voice sounded very strained, his tone very guarded, as I imagined his captors were monitoring the call. "You will have to come over," he said gravely. "Lt. ___ will pick you up. Something happened. Princess is here with me."

In a nondescript office in Camp Crame—made more eerie because it was almost midnight—Dodong and Princess made me sit between them, each of them holding one of my hands as a number of intelligence officers showed me some very gruesome pictures of two decomposing bodies. They were trying to identify the bodies, they said, and they had reason to believe that the two were our friends. Had I heard from them at all within the last three days?

My brother pressed my hand, signaling me to be careful and sparing with information. I hadn't, I truthfully answered. I had not seen or heard from anyone in my brother's group since they were captured. (Isolating family members of recent captures was SOP among the hunted.)

When the interrogators left us alone for a few minutes, probably because they sensed my great distress, my brother was able to whisper to me. "I'm afraid something tragic has happened to the people in my group. Please try to contact them." I knew that it pained him to ask me to do that because he had wanted to shield me from the danger of being a military suspect. But he had no other contact with the outside world.

The next few days were a living hell. I was able to find Jack and together we made calls, visited homes, and searched all the possible places. Nothing. Since most of the people we were looking for were in hiding, their families heard from them only sporadically and were no help. Bit by little bit, after painstaking work, we were able to get a trickle of information on when most of them were last seen. They were on their way to a location in Central Luzon, summoned to a meeting by party leaders. From there, the trail went cold.

A few days later, my brother told me that the military had identified the two bodies: Omar Verdote and a certain Ka Popoy, both assassinated by someone they must have known. The news hit me like a bullet in the heart. The two were very close to me and I was counting on them to protect me, and my brother's children, from harm.

Eventually, Jack and I found Art, who was supposed to have been part of that group that was summoned for the meeting but wasn't able to go because he was sick.

Weeks later, a clearer picture emerged. It was a mass assassination ordered by the people who our friends looked up to as their leaders. Among the victims were Rene Miranda, Ray Fragante, a certain Roger "Putol" and others whose names escape me now. All were wrongly accused of betraying the revolution by people who eventually surrendered to Marcos. All died in their prime.

For those who escaped the ultimate betrayal, it was an excruciatingly painful period. We grieved for a long time, for our friends, for the loss of our innocence. It was not supposed to end that way.

We were so young then . . .

•*Filipinas* Magazine, June 1999 •

EDSA Is a Terrible Thing to Waste

WHERE WERE you this same month in 1986 when the motherland unexpectedly and peacefully ousted an ailing and overstaying head of state, earning the country the respect of the world and giving a previously cowed people a sense of its own collective power?

Has it really been seventeen years since the "EDSA People Power Revolution," the three-day event that was sparked by what we now know as a failed coup and ended with dancing in the streets in celebration of a new leader, a new government and a whole bundle of unrealistic expectations?

It was an entire lifetime ago, for many of us. Since then many of the heroes of EDSA have morphed into insufferable villains, not much different (in some instances, even worse) than those we tagged as enemies then. And a few of those "enemies" have turned out, on closer inspection, as better human beings than those whom we hailed as saviors.

The major participants of EDSA 1986 scrambled for historical credit for making it happen. The Cory forces, for example, claimed that without Cory Aquino's courage to fight Ferdinand Marcos in a lopsided electoral battle, there would not have been an EDSA. The RAM boys, drunk with their own sense of invincibility, insisted it was they who did it. The Catholic Church said it was a miracle; the Left, which stoked the fires of protest even when the Marcos regime was at the peak of its power but which was tragically marginalized during his actual fall, said EDSA was brought about by revolutionary fervor. Others pointed to the CIA as the behind-the-scenes prodder and financier, which prompted the "Ninoy" forces and the military rebels to action.

All of them are correct, and all of them are wrong. EDSA 1986 was a glorious moment in our country's history because it was like a cacophony of disparate orchestras finally melding into one, a rare confluence of previously conflicting forces unified, albeit too briefly, in the pursuit of a common goal. An alignment of planets, in cosmic terms; a once-in-a-lifetime occurrence.

As such, not one group or individual can claim ascendancy and certainly the concept of a miracle (admittedly quite a romantic notion) is bogus because it does not take into account the long and painful historical processes that were in motion long before the culmination known as EDSA 1986.

It has become more difficult to recall the glory of EDSA 1986 because of the murkiness and frustrations that have dominated the Philippine scene since then. I have to dust off my books to recapture the sense of wonder that we all had when we stood *kapit-bisig* with friends and strangers those February days when our optimism was intact and our determination unabashed.

But I am glad that I have the EDSA 1986 experience to draw upon when many things in our home country seem to be going wrong. And, judging from the number of people who want to leave the homeland (one out of five Filipinos, according to a survey), there are a lot of things going wrong or about to go wrong. Which makes me wonder if the concept of EDSA—or the bastardization of it—is contributing somewhat to the national malaise.

The EDSA of our collective consciousness, a friend commented, is an effective way of getting rid of an unacceptable president but it does not teach the people anything about respect for institutions and governance. While it has raised the national self-esteem by empowering the people against abuse and corruption, it has also made people less patient with or uninterested in the excruciatingly slow and tedious work that a functioning democracy requires.

The multiple coup attempts against the Cory administration were classic examples of the dark side of the EDSA concept. Instead of being able to harness the government's assets and resources to move the country forward, the administration had to use them to ward off the six or so attempts to topple it. Even now, three presidents and more than a decade later, the country is still a powder keg which could explode with just the slightest destabilization moves.

Just imagine, if the spirit of unity and togetherness that characterized EDSA 1986 could be harnessed for nation-building and progress, what great strides the Philippines would make in getting out of the rut and despair it is in. Imagine, if all the contentious groups would say, okay, let's put aside our differences first and each of us do our part in alleviating our people's misery, how much energy and resources could be freed up and redirected towards ensuring a better life for all. Imagine, if all Filipinos in the Philippines and elsewhere would do their part in rebuilding instead of finger-pointing or simply not caring, how much could collectively be accomplished for the motherland.

Naïve and idealistic, you say? But I experienced EDSA 1986 and I saw clearly the heights our people were capable of reaching. As I think back on that watershed event, I am still amazed at the collective will that transformed what was potentially a very violent situation into one that was peaceful, and very Filipino. Since then, I've told myself never to distrust the Filipino people again, a promise that admittedly had been sorely tested.

The columnist Conrad de Quiros said it best in his Dec. 20, 2002 piece: "… our problem was never that we were incapable of heroic action, as witness the bursts of people power. It is that we are incapable of sustaining it, as witness our lapsing into mediocrity afterward."

Here's hoping we prove ourselves better next time around.

(The ouster of Joseph Estrada, now known as EDSA 2, did not get quite as broad a support as the first EDSA, as attested to by the revolt of the Erap masses a few months later.)

• *Filipinas* Magazine, February 2003 •

The Other Side of EDSA

SHORTLY AFTER the People Power Revolution, a.k.a. EDSA One, in February 1986, I was asked to co-author a book that would document the Marcos years. My assigned chapter was the period that began with the Snap Elections and ended with the triumph at EDSA. The book, *Dictatorship and Revolution: Roots of People's Power*, was a historical researcher's delight, an exceptionally comprehensive tome that included a lot of supporting documents.

For my chapter, I interviewed a lot of the personalities and groups that participated in the events that led to the downfall of Marcos. They were a varied lot: in addition to the major players, I chased after military officers, government officials of both the Marcos and the Aquino administrations, activists, religious leaders, U.S. Embassy officials, media personalities and politicians. My intention was to piece together as complete a story as possible from various angles of that momentous time in the country's history.

There was a glaring omission in my piece, however. I wasn't able to get the real story of what actually happened in Malacañang at that time since that side's major players had already left the country. All I could do was glean from press reports and Monday morning quarterbacking. No "I was there" account, just maybes, and wild guesses.

At the time I was writing it, I didn't think the gap in my story was crucial. Just like everyone else who was caught up in the euphoria of the moment, I considered the Marcos camp the enemy that was finally accorded its just desserts. Just like everyone else who was personally victimized by martial law, I demonized Marcos and everyone associated with him. No attempt at journalistic or historical objectivity could make me change my mind.

But time, distance, a less confrontational world view, and the disappointments about the real character and motives of some of the EDSA "heroes" have a way of piercing through one's blinders and tempering one's self-righteousness. When I met some of the fellow exiles of the Marcoses here in San Francisco, I asked them, out of curiosity, to tell me their stories. When I put together in my mind the tapestry that was EDSA, what emerged was a very human drama of cues and miscues, of heroics and betrayals, of brilliance and blunders.

Here are some interesting behind the scenes stories that I didn't get the first time around, as told by those who lived through them:

The Presidential Security Group (PSG) uncovered the coup plot of the Reform the Armed Forces Movement (RAM) as early as December 1985 when they sent two of their own to "infiltrate" the ranks of the plotters. However, no attempt was made to stop the plot because no one had broken the law yet. The strategy was to clandestinely monitor the RAM's activities, consolidate the defense of Malacañang (thus the numerous batallions that surrounded the Palace when EDSA happened), and, as zero hour drew near, arrest the key operatives. Which was exactly what happened.

The arrest of Captain Ricardo Morales, a highly regarded aide to the First Lady, was a drama in itself. Morales was on leave from his duties due to schooling and was not physically reporting to the PSG. So when he appeared there the morning of February 21, 1986, those who saw him were surprised and alerted. They monitored his movements and took note when he asked that a gun be issued to him. As he was about to leave the place, Col. Arturo Aruiza called him into his office "to chat." There he was confronted by Col. Irwin Ver, then commander of the Presidential

Guards, who told him that they knew of the plot and that he, Morales, was part of it. Morales responded by asking for a lawyer.

Aruiza got so angry at what he considered Morales's admission of guilt that he left the room to get his gun. Had Ver not caught Aruiza's intent, and ordered, "*Walang mamamatay dito* (No one is going to be killed here)," the result would have been tragic. Morales's arrest was only confirmed by the RAM boys when he was presented on TV during Marcos's press conference on the night Enrile and Ramos declared their break from the president. It sent shivers down the spine of those who knew the crucial role Morales was supposed to have played during the planned assault on the Palace: To lead Honasan and his men to the private quarters of the Marcoses.

In the months preceding EDSA, Marcos was so seriously ill that he only had a 2-3 hour window for official functions each day before he would be taken away to rest. When he was informed of the coup plot, he tasked Irwin Ver to research military history and strategies, and spent an hour each day discussing these with him. As D-day drew near, Marcos asked for details of the defensive positions, the cover and concealment strategies, and even the names of the soldiers at the forefront. "His mind was still very sharp," Ver recalls.

On the second day of EDSA I, Malacañang was informed that the Enrile/Ramos forces would initiate military action (which turned out to be false) so the Marines with their tanks and armored vehicles were sent to surround Camp Aguinaldo as a preventive measure. That was when the famous Kodak moments of the "miracle of EDSA" happened, when nuns knelt in front of the tanks and people offered flowers to the soldiers before the troops withdrew. While there would be no denying the effect of such a lovefest on the soldiers' will to fight, the withdrawal was actually ordered by Marcos when he woke up that day. The president thought any military action was unnecessary because he was confident he could talk Johnny and Eddie out of their madness. He also downplayed the significance of the mass action at EDSA and was confident that his administration would prevail with the unwavering support of the United States.

Adamantly refusing the frantic advice of his military council to order aggressive military action against the rebel forces, Marcos decided to move his government to Ilocos. It was a hasty retreat. Within two hours, the First Family had vacated the Palace and U.S. Air Force helicopters airlifted them to Clark Air Base. Upon reaching Pampanga, Marcos wanted to proceed immediately to Paoay but Gen. Allen, the American base commander, opposed the night flight, citing safety concerns.

Before turning in that night in Clark, General Fabian Ver ordered the movement of AFP divisions north of the Agno river, and a blocking force composed of the First Army Division was set up in Tarlac. Two Armed Forces were about to be formed, two Philippine governments were to be established, a civil war loomed in the horizon.

At dawn, Gen. Allen informed Marcos that their aircrafts were ready. It was unclear whether Marcos understood that he was being flown out of the country, or if he was tricked into flying, thinking he was going to his home province. Considerably weakened by the day's events, Marcos was strapped to a bed throughout the flight. By morning, he woke up to a rainy day in Guam, while the Filipinos reveled in a majestic Manila sunrise.

• *Filipinas* Magazine, February 2004 •

The End of Her World

OF THE MANY unusual things that happened on the day her world collapsed, she remembers most the sunshine, so piercing bright that it shone through the opaque *capiz* window that held the dust of decades, into the greenish blue mosquito net that shrouded her bed, waking her up before her usual hour. The only other time she experienced such brightness was when she was in labor with her son, her only child, twenty-three years prior. That was the happiest day of her life.

But on the day her world collapsed, the bright sunshine also brought an ache in her chest that she never felt before. It was not the wild-horses-stomping kind of pain that she would have recognized as a heart attack. Neither was it the neither-here-nor-there kind of pain that usually accompanied indigestion. Rather, it was a just-there ache that did not stop her from doing the things she did throughout the day, yet insinuated itself enough for her to be conscious of its ebbing and flowing as the hours ticked by.

Just as she would every morning upon waking, she prayed the rosary on her knees and prostrated herself in front of the foot-high crucifix that she had adorned the afternoon before with fresh *sampaguita, kalachuchi* and *ilang-ilang* blooms stringed together with abaca thread. She had always loved the combined fragrance of these flowers, the pungent scent of *ilang-ilang* tempered by the gentle sweetness of the other two. That morning she noticed that the smell of the *kalachuchi* seemed dominant, making her think for a few seconds of death and funerals.

Just as she did each time she prayed, she pleaded for the safety of her son, her only child, the only family she had left since her husband died shortly after their beloved *unico hijo* left to pursue the passion of his soul. News of the father's death did not reach the son until much later, months in fact. She was quite angry about his very obvious absence, stumbling over the empty excuses that she managed to conjure to explain his inexplicable transgression of filial piety.

One night when a typhoon was lashing the province and the rain that was pouring in torrents muffled the sound of barking dogs and masked the silence of night, her son came home. He was wearing the same denim jeans and checkered shirt he wore when he said goodbye to her, but this time his clothes hung loosely on his clearly thinned body. He was soaked and hungry, disconsolate over his father's demise and apologetic for the stress that his mother had to endure alone. They prayed together and talked through the night, the son explaining the harsh realities of the world to the mother who had lived through those realities every single day of her life. At dawn, he was gone.

She would receive letters from him. They would always be on onionskin sheet, small and folded so tightly, his handwriting changed so drastically by the need to put so many words and thoughts in so little space. He wrote of how happy and fulfilled he felt doing what he chose to do, how harsh were the problems of the common folk, how he had come to know the terrain of the land and the language of the clouds. There was no rhyme nor rhythm to the appearance of his letters. Sometimes she would receive two in a week, other times she would not hear from him for months. She never really knew how his letters would reach her; it was almost like they appeared from nowhere and they would define the fullness or emptiness of her days as she read and reread them, savoring his virtual presence, never wanting to let go until the next one came.

One day, he wrote that he had fallen in love and had been wed in a ceremony witnessed by a very few. The wife, he said, was somebody she would love instantly as the daughter she never had. He promised that they would visit the first chance they get, perhaps shortly before they would be presenting her with the grandchild she had been hoping for. She had looked forward to that day and had busied herself with sewing blankets and clothes for the little one. She had even checked on her next-door neighbor, the midwife, to make sure she would be available at a moment's notice, just in case the birthing would take place at her house.

On the day her world collapsed, she felt the tug in her stomach that always signaled, to her mind, the unexpected, and she was almost sure it was the day her new family would be complete. She waited impatiently for dusk, when the entire town would light up their *gaseras* (oil lamps) and shut their windows, the perfect time for her son and his wife to slip surreptitiously into her house. So confident was she that it was the night of their coming that she kept the *tinolang manok* (ginger chicken soup), his favorite dish, warming in the *palayok* (clay pot) so they could sit right down as soon as they arrived.

She waited that night, like any parent would, for a child coming home from war. Not wanting to waste a moment to open the door, she sat on her rocking chair, her senses alert to the ticking of the minutes and the sounds of the night. She would nod off to sleep occasionally but would always catch herself and wake up. She never, for a second, allowed herself to think that they wouldn't come because as a mother, she knew that her son would once again fill her world with his presence.

When dawn came, a neighbor knocked on her door. Come quickly, he told her, there was someone at his house who wanted to talk to her. The roosters were crowing and the sky was already displaying the orange of sunrise when she was told the news: Her son and his wife, along with the much longed for grandchild in the womb, were felled by gunshots as they tried to elude their hunters. It happened just two barrios away, shortly after dusk, at the time she was warming the *tinolang manok* for their supper.

The couple, she later learned, had turned their backs on the war they were fighting and were going home to her.

• *Filipinas* Magazine, October 2004 •

Secrets and Lies

HOW MANY TIMES in our lifetime are we told this cliché, or a variation of it. Let it go, don't rock the boat, don't exhume old wounds, get over it. Let sleeping dogs lie.

Often these are said as acts of kindness or consideration, as when one tries to dredge up a family scandal and the participants or victims are still around. *Pabayaan mo na,* our elders would admonish, thus sweeping all queries and speculations under the rug, along with the lessons that may have been gleaned from the experience.

But what if the situation that is being covered up is a national tragedy or a hideous crime that involves multiple betrayals and deaths? Should the principle of "let sleeping dogs lie" apply when to do so would mean not just distorting history but also robbing people of the chance to learn from and prevent another travesty? The logical answer, the civilized answer, is no, yet the history of the world is replete with such lapses.

In the past few decades in the Philippines, two such historical abominations stand out: The Jabidah massacre in 1968, where more than thirty Muslim recruits for a clandestine military action called Oplan Merdeka were executed in their training camp in Corregidor; and the Plaza Miranda bombing of 1971, where almost the entire senatorial slate of the Liberal Party were wounded (some seriously and permanently) and nine bystanders were killed when two grenades were lobbed at their *miting de avance*.

The Marcos military tried to cover up the 1968 tragedy and would have succeeded were it not for the doggedness of then-opposition senator Benigno Aquino who spearheaded the investigation and initiated congressional hearings that led to the court martial of eight officers and 16 enlisted men that same year. The investigation and court case never yielded anything conclusive about the motive for the operation, however, and those charged with the crime were acquitted in 1971.

What really happened in Corregidor in 1968 would have forever remained in the dustbin of history had it not been for two ace women journalists, Marites Danguilan-Vitug and Glenda Gloria, whose interest in Mindanao and the long-running Muslim rebellion there were honed by extensive research. In seeking an answer to the "why" of the southern insurrection, the two courageous women were brought back to the Jabidah massacre which, they realized, was "the spark that lit the Muslim rebellion, the Plaza Miranda of Mindanao."

In their excellent book, *Under the Crescent Moon: Rebellion in Mindanao*, which probably comes closest to the truth about Oplan Merdeka, they wrote: "Only a small group in the Armed Forces may have been involved in Operation Merdeka but it tainted the reputation of the AFP. To this day, it is kept as a dark secret which many in the military refuse to talk about."

Marcos blamed the Communist Party (CPP) for the Plaza Miranda bombing and used it as the reason to suspend the writ of habeas corpus in 1971, and the declaration of martial law in 1972. Nobody believed him. His radical measures to curtail the communist insurgency (and not coincidentally, ensure his stay in power) ironically led to the widespread radicalization of many young men and women. In the last few years of his twenty-year rule, the ranks of the New People's Army (NPA) grew from a ragtag group of around two hundred confined in Isabela, to around fifteen thousand guerillas operating nationwide.

In one of the Marcos jails shortly after martial law was declared, however, the whispers among CPP insiders was too shocking to make public, too painful to accept. The scuttlebutt was that it was, in fact, the top officials of the CPP who ordered the Plaza Miranda bombing. An NPA operative, Danny Cordero, had sworn to this shortly before he was executed in the hinterlands of Isabela by the head of the NPA in the area. Cordero's alleged crime (according to those in the group who tried to stop his unjustified execution), was insubordination or disloyalty. His futile defense in a nutshell: "How can I be accused of being disloyal when I (with two others, one who lobbed the second grenade and the other who engineered their getaway) carried out the order to bomb Plaza Miranda?"

After Marcos was overthrown, some of those who heard Cordero's confession went public with their knowledge. As expected, they were excoriated by many who insisted (but could not present any proof) that it was Marcos's henchmen who did it. Privately, they were taken to task by their comrades. Let sleeping dogs lie, they were warned. After all, the perpetrators are all dead. Just bury the past under piles of holier-than-thou rhetoric and noble intentions.

The ghost of Plaza Miranda was exhumed recently with the assassination of ex-NPA chief Rolly Kintanar by his former comrades. As Nathan Quimpo, a retired CPP ideologue, wrote in the *Inquirer*, the real reasons for Kintanar's liquidation were because he knew too much (about party operations) and he dared oppose (the party higher-ups). One of his "sins," according to Quimpo, could have been that Kintanar had strongly proposed an inside investigation of the Plaza Miranda bombing and was strongly rebuffed by party officials. Kintanar was in Isabela when the Danny Cordero confession took place.

One despicable tragedy that decimated the ranks of the leftist rebels throughout the 1980s was the *Kampanyang Ahos* in Mindanao and its Southern Tagalog equivalent, Oplan Missing Link. The goal was to purge the organization of hundreds of suspected deep penetration agents (DPAs) and it resulted in the torture and execution of hundreds of its members based on what was eventually proven to be flimsy evidence. The organizational shame would have led to organizational amnesia (many of those who survived were reportedly so traumatized that they could not muster the words to talk about their experience) were it not for a small group of victims who have come out publicly to tell their stories.

In his deeply touching, extremely riveting book, *To Suffer Thy Comrades*, Robert Francis Garcia wrote about his horrifying experience at the hands of his comrades and that of several others who have chosen to go public in an effort not only to achieve personal closure but to understand why people betray and why people torture.

It is a must-read, for students of Philippine history and organizational psychology, and for those who need to realize that to let sleeping dogs lie is to risk having them wake up and bite us again and again.

• *Filipinas* Magazine, March 2003 •

Through Dark Glasses, Brightly

OKAY, enough already!

The developments in the Philippines in the past few months have raised the volume of whining among those who still genuinely care, whether they be in the country or abroad. Indeed, if one takes several steps back and look at the forest instead of the trees, one can see that Filipinos, wherever they may be based, are united in their worry and despair over the future of our homeland. And it's easy to see why.

The political circus has arrived and the acts are not exactly enticing, to say the least. Between an ineffectual incumbent wounded by charges of corruption within her inner circle, a popular movie actor with no experience in governing a large-scale production like running a country, a military man-turned-politician who is reputed to be a drug lord cum killer and a bureaucrat/politician devoid of the common touch, there is hardly any reason for excitement. Add to the mix the cabal of opportunists and criminals that dot the Philippine political scene today and it is easy to see how one can readily identify with the°twenty percent of Filipinos who want to leave the country and the millions who have left and are thanking their lucky stars that they have done so.

Where are the Jose Rizals, the Gabriela Silangs, the Andres Bonifacios among us, we lament. Are there no Ghandis or Martin Luther Kings or Nelson Mandelas in our midst who can inspire and unite? Can't our nation produce a Lee Kuan Yew, a Mahathir, a Ho Chi Minh or even a Mao—personalities so big they were able to pull an entire country towards a vision that transcended the pettiness of minor functionaries and the superficiality of the politics-of-the-moment? Is it our destiny as a people to be fractured and impoverished? Are we being punished for our sins? Do we have to be constantly betrayed by those who claim to want the best for us?

We can go on and on with our litany of what-ifs and what-should-have-beens but all it will do is drag us deeper into despair and cynicism—twin emotions that are counterproductive and incredibly debilitating. So why don't we try something novel and look at the positives instead? The half-full glass versus the half-empty, the sunshine over the clouds.

From the prism of an eternal optimist, here's what I think we should celebrate:

- The Philippines remains a democracy. Flawed and profane, true, but a living one, despite the attempts by certain ambitious sectors to curtail our people's freedom in the name of law and order or economic progress. Those among us who are overly critical of our motherland because it is not like the United States should keep this in mind. The nation is still young, it is still in the process of evolution. If we look at the histories of the great nations of the world fifty-seven years after their founding, we will realize that they too went through the noise and the chaos that our homeland is going through right now. Those Southeast Asian countries that have become economic tigers are not democracies. Whether the Philippines should follow their lead—give up democracy in exchange for order and economic progress—is another issue altogether.

- Elections, not revolution. The gap between rich and poor is wider than ever but the Filipino people continue to invest their hope in elections as the avenue for change (well, also as a source of personal income). We have the longest-running multiple insurgencies, which have drained our national coffers and stymied progress, yet these insurgencies have remained on the fringe because the people as a whole still prefer peace to war.

- The underground economy remains robust. We who have forgotten how it is to live in the Philippines wonder how the people survive in the face of economic woes. The hard life has made the Filipino "*maabilidad*." Remember the panties and *longganisa* peddled to office workers during lunch hour? The sticks of banana cue that schoolchildren sell to their classmates? The boys who weave through vehicles to clean the windows of those stopped in traffic? The heritage of smallness, as Nick Joaquin wrote, is what keeps the ordinary Filipino, with no visible regular wage, afloat.

- The Filipinos' resiliency and humor are unbeatable. A survey has revealed that Filipinos are the happiest people in Asia. In another survey, more than seventy percent of Filipinos say that they are happy with their love lives. Despite the hardships that our countrymen have to endure, they continue to hope and dream and sing and laugh. If you doubt this, just look at the karaoke bars and the text messages. *O, di ba?*

- Camaraderie lives. Why do those who go home regularly enjoy their time there immensely? We may have all the creature comforts here but it is back home where we enjoy the *samahan* (kinship) and *barkadahan* (camaraderie). Humidity and mosquitoes notwithstanding, we crave and savor the unity of spirit that we can only get there.

- Never a dull moment. My friends back home are amazed at how we expats plan our lives way in advance. This is something they can't do because between natural disasters and political upheavals, there is no such thing as predictability of life. The country never lacks for O'Henry-like twists and that's what makes living there exciting, if sometimes dangerous. And oh yes, exasperating. But never ever boring.

So the next time you are tempted to bellyache and despair, consider looking at things from the other side. Because deep inside us we know that clowns and presidents may come and go but our homeland and our people will endure.

• *Filipinas* Magazine, January 2004 •

GEMMA NEMENZO is Managing Editor and columnist of *Filipinas*, the only monthly glossy magazine for the Filipino American community circulated in all fifty U.S. states. Before she moved to the San Francisco Bay Area with her three children in 1988, she was a freelance journalist writing for various publications in Manila. She was also part of the pioneering team that conceptualized and created *Batibot*, the acclaimed children's educational TV show. A journalism graduate of the University of the Philippines, Gemma has had extensive experience writing for both television and print. In the U.S., she worked for more than ten years as an abstractor/editor for a major electronic database publisher. Her popular column, Slant, appears monthly in *Filipinas Magazine*.